The 500 Hidden Secrets of

ANTWERP

INTRODUCTION

This is a guide to the Antwerp that almost no one knows. It takes you off the beaten track to discover the city's hidden gardens, unknown museums and small coffee bars. In these pages, you will find the 5 best places to eat frites, the 5 museums that no one should miss and the 5 best independent record shops in town.

The aim is to take the reader to unexpected places that are different in some way from the normal tourist destinations. With this book tucked in your pocket, you can set out to find secret atomic bunkers, a vine that has been growing since the 16th century and a railway station that was moved 36 metres by rail. You will also be guided to a café terrace on top of a grain silo, a cinema located in a former police station and a collection of 17 historic cranes.

The book is also a guide to some of the more unusual experiences that you can track down in Antwerp. So you can find out where to eat the best dim sum in Chinatown, sample a chocolate flavoured with fried bacon and plunge into a swimming pool moored in the river.

This book doesn't mention everything there is to see in Antwerp. There are already enough guide books and websites that cover the familiar sights. The aim here is to create an intimate guide to the places the author would recommend to a friend who wanted to discover the real Antwerp.

HOW TO USE
THIS BOOK?

This book contains 500 things about Antwerp in 100 different categories. Some are places to visit. Others are random bits of information. The aim is to inspire, not to cover the city from A to Z.

The places listed in the guide are given an address, a district and a number. The district and number allow you to find the locations on the maps.

You need to bear in mind that cities change all the time. The chef who hits a high note one day can be uninspiring on the day you happen to visit. The hotel ecstatically reviewed in this book might suddenly decline under a new manager. The bar considered one of the 5 best places for live music might be empty on the night you visit.

This is obviously a highly personal selection. You might not always agree with it. If you want to leave a comment, recommend a bar or reveal your favourite place, you can contact the publisher at info@uitgeverijluster.be or post a message on the author's website www.mysecretantwerp.com.

THE AUTHOR

Derek Blyth has lived in Belgium for more than 20 years. As a journalist, he has explored almost every corner of the country. He first visited Antwerp in 1989 and wrote extensively about the city in 1993 when it was cultural capital of Europe.

Formerly editor of the Brussels English-language weekly *The Bulletin*, he has written several books on the Low Countries, including *Flemish Cities Explored* and *Brussels for Pleasure*. He is also co-founder of the discussion forum Café Europa. In 2012, he published a guide to *The 500 Hidden Secrets of Brussels*. An instant bestseller, it was praised for showing people a side of the city they never knew existed.

In drawing up this list of 500 hidden secrets of Antwerp, the author was helped and advised by friends, journalists and local historians. He is particularly grateful to Nadine Malfait for a long walk around Borgerhout and a pile of books on the city, Hadewijch Ceulemans for her insider addresses, David Flamée at MoMu for fashion briefings, Stéphanie Duval for cool addresses in the city she likes to call 'the new Paris' and Eva Heynen for a little bottle of Elixir d'Anvers.

He would also like to thank publisher Marc Verhagen for his warm support, photographer Joram Van Holen for capturing the cool essence of Antwerp, Hadewijch Ceulemans for steering the project to completion, and typographer Joke Gossé for patiently putting together a beautiful book. And, lastly, thanks as always to Mary for her support.

ANTWERP:
overview

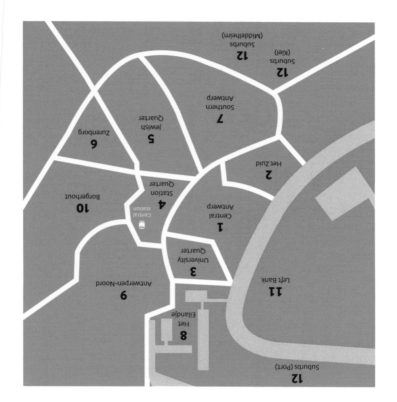

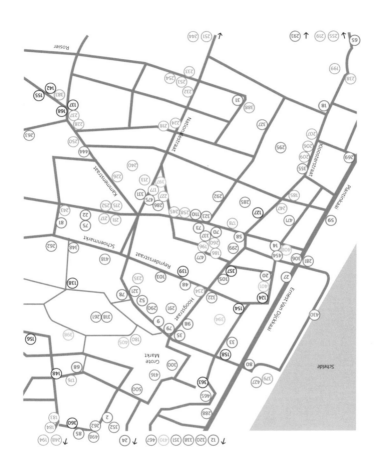

CENTRAL ANTWERP
Map 1

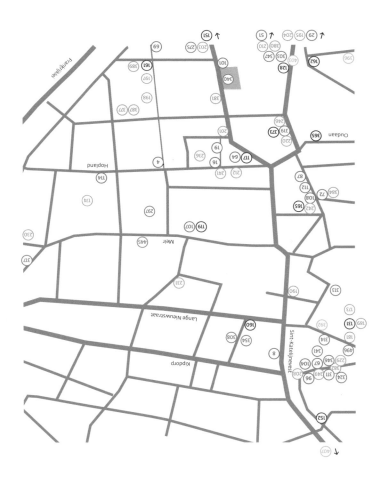

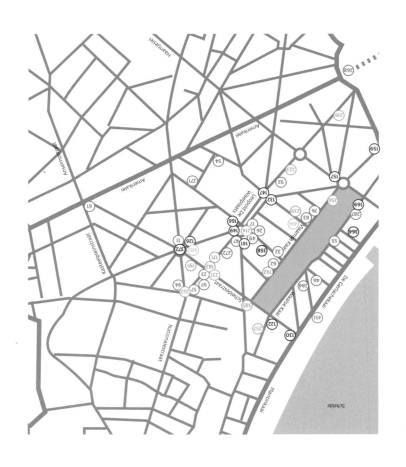

Map 2
HET ZUID

Map 3
UNIVERSITY QUARTER

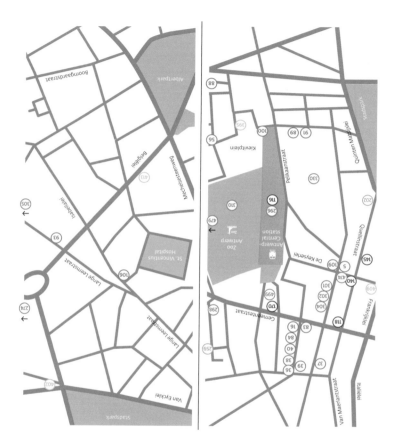

Map 4
STATION
QUARTER

Map 5
JEWISH
QUARTER

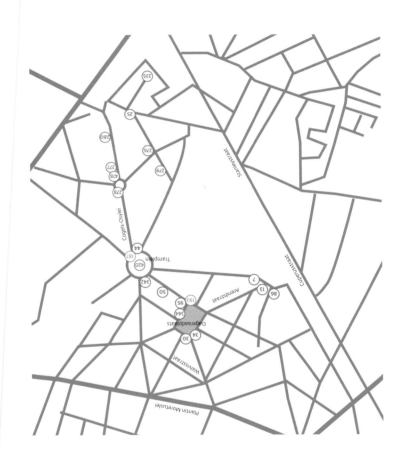

Map 6

ZURENBORG

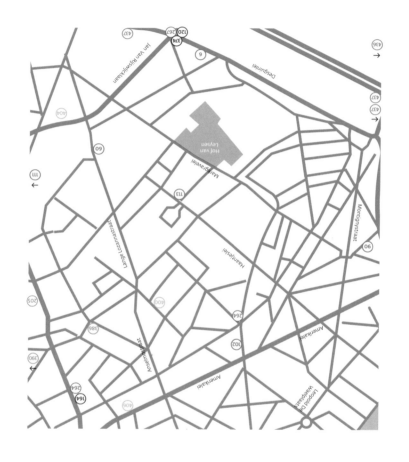

Map 7
SOUTHERN ANTWERP

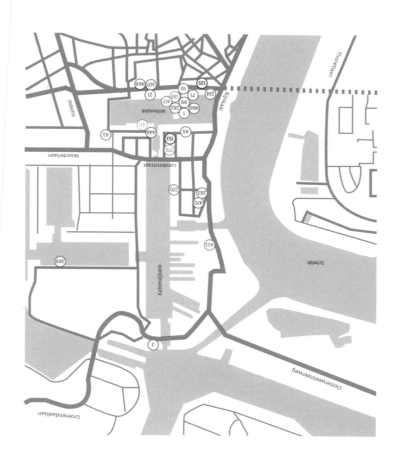

Map 8
HET EILANDJE

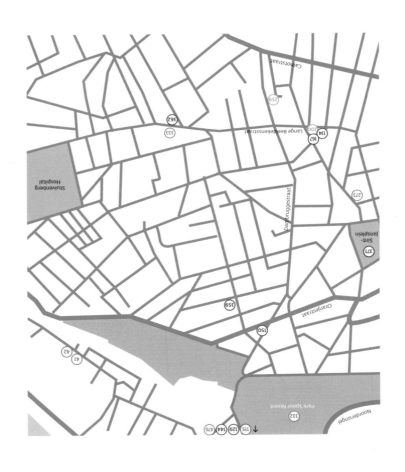

ANTWERPEN-NOORD

Map 9

Map 10

BORGERHOUT

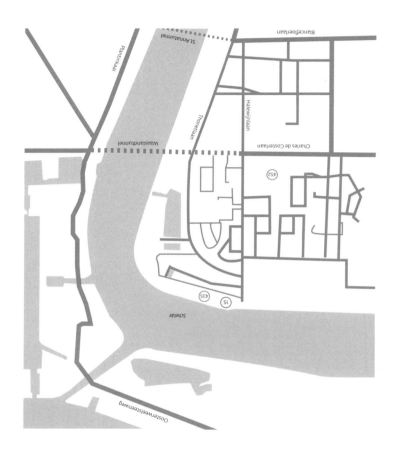

Map 11
LEFT BANK

Map 12
SUBURBS

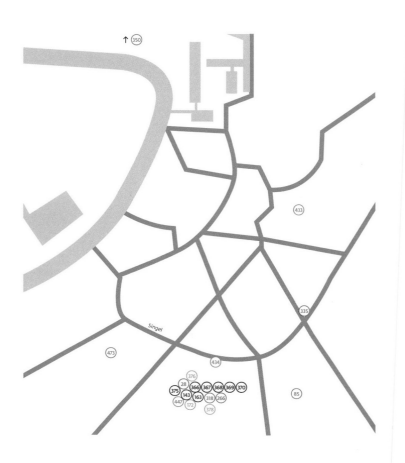

MADEMOISELLE MOUSTACHE

115 PLACES
TO EAT GOOD FOOD

The 5 most
BEAUTIFUL
RESTAURANTS

1 **'T ZILTE**
   Hanzestedenplaats 5
   Het Eilandje ⑧
   +32 (0)3 283 40 40
   www.tzilte.be

Located on the ninth floor of Antwerp's city museum, 't Zilte is run by one of the best chefs in the country. Viki Geunes used to own a restaurant in Mol, but moved his staff to this dazzling new location in 2011. The 17 cooks employed in the kitchen ensure that the food is visually stunning and constantly innovative. Closed at weekends.

2 **HOFSTRAAT 24**
   Hofstraat 24
   Central Antwerp ①
   +32 (0)3 225 05 45
   www.hofstraat24.be

Here is one of the most civilised places to eat in the heart of the old town. It occupies a 16th century coach house that was restored by the interior designer Axel Vervoordt to create three separate dining areas. You can choose between a sober modern room with a splashy abstract painting, a brighter conservatory or a secluded library with just two tables. While the menu is limited, the cooking is faultless.

3 **HET POMPHUIS**
Siberiastraat
Het Eilandje ⑧
+32 (0)3 770 86 25
www.hetpomphuis.be

In 2002 this imposing restaurant opened in the port area. You may need a car or taxi to get out here, but it is worth the effort to eat in this industrial monument from 1920. While waiting for the food to arrive, you can admire shiny pumps that could empty a dock in two hours and watch huge Chinese container ships slide past the windows. The cooking here is serious and professional.

4 **HORTA**
Hopland 2
Central Antwerp ①
+ 32 (0)3 232 28 15
www.grandcafehorta.be

This spectacular brasserie was constructed using fragments of Victor Horta's Maison du Peuple. The Art Nouveau masonry and ironwork were salvaged and fragments were incorporated into this grand café. The walls are hung with architect's plans and nostalgic photographs of the building. A stylish place to sample hearty Flemish dishes.

5 **GRAN DUCA**
De Keyserlei 28
Station Quarter ④
+32 (0)3 202 68 87
www.granduca.be

Here is an Italian restaurant that you will not stumble upon by chance. You find it by going down a narrow passage decorated with murals of Italian cities and taking a lift to the sixth floor. This brings you to a hidden rooftop restaurant above the Hylitt Hotel. The menu offers a small range of authentic Italian dishes like saltimbocca di vitello and tagliatelle ai funghi di bosco. But the main attraction is the rooftop deck where you can eat out in the summer surrounded by lavender bushes.

The 5 restaurants for
EXCEPTIONAL COOKING

---

6 **RADIS-NOIR**

Desguinlei 186
Southern Antwerp ②
+32 (0)3 238 37 70
www.radisnoir.be

It may not look particularly impressive, but this is a hidden gem. The chef Jo Bussels has created an exceptional restaurant where everything is just right, from the inventive cooking to the friendly atmosphere. Booking is essential, even on a rainy Monday in November.

7 **DÔME**

Grote Hondstraat 2
Zurenborg ⑥
+32 (0)3 239 90 03
www.domeweb.be

This used to be a tea room before it was transformed by architect Paul Wauters and stylist Sophie Verbeke. They carefully preserved the interior with its beautiful mosaic floor and impressive neo-classical domed ceiling to create a grand restaurant. Here you can discover the cooking talents of Julien Burlat, an award-winning chef from Lyon.

8 DE GODEVAART

Sint-Katelijnevest 23
Central Antwerp ①
+32 (0)3 231 89 94
www.degodevaart.be

This is a beautiful restaurant in an old part of town with a quiet courtyard at the back where vines grow up the walls. The young chef Dave De Belder likes to experiment with new ideas in his kitchen, but he also spends time hunting out the very best ingredients. He presents his cooking in a series of menus, ranging from three to seven courses.

9 SIR ANTHONY VAN DIJCK

Oude Koornmarkt 16
Central Antwerp ①
+32 (0)3 231 61 70
www.siranthonyvandijck.be

Named after the 17th century painter, Sir Anthony van Dijck is hidden down a narrow cobbled lane. Opened by chef Marc Paesbrugghe in 1975, this quickly became one of the best restaurants in town with two Michelin stars to its name. Then Paesbrugghe astonished everyone in 1992 by handing back the stars so he could concentrate on honest cooking. Paesbrugghe follows the French tradition, although the setting is pure Flemish baroque.

10 MARCEL

Van Schoonbekeplein 13
Het Eilandje ⑧
+32 (0)3 336 33 02
www.restaurantmarcel.be

Marcel occupies a handsome 1912 building that was once a seamen's mission run by the Dawson Memorial Church. The building was recently restored to create a stylish restaurant furnished in the style of a 1920s Parisian brasserie. The chef offers a classic French-style menu based on the best ingredients he can find.

The 5 best restaurants for
FISH FROM THE NORTH SEA

11 **FISKEBAR**
Marnixplaats 11
Het Zuid ②
+32 (0)3 257 13 57
www.fiskebar.be

Here is a beautiful Scandinavian-style fish restaurant with simple white tiled walls. You sit in straight rows at small tables. The menu is chalked on a blackboard. The chef Nicolai Kovdal takes the freshest fish he can find and cooks it to perfection. You can order lobster, grilled sole or calamari, or opt for the *plateau fruits de mer*.

12 **DOCK'S CAFÉ**
Jordaenskaai 7
Central Antwerp ①
+32 (0)3 226 63 30
www.docks.be

This big modern brasserie opened on the Scheldt waterfront in 1991. The designer Antoine Pinto created a dramatic industrial interior with a sweeping staircase that fitted the mood of the 1990s.

13 **DÔME SUR MER**
Arendstraat 1
Zurenborg ⑥
+32 (0)3 281 74 33
www.domeweb.be

The people behind Dôme have created a fish restaurant in the hip Zurenborg district. It has a clean white interior with a long goldfish tank set in the wall. You can drop in here for a simple dish of oysters and a glass of white wine or spend an entire evening working through the seafood menu.

14 HET NIEUWE PALINGHUIS

Sint-Jansvliet 14
Central Antwerp ①
+32 (0)3 231 74 45
www.hetnieuwepalinghuis.be

This is a traditional Belgian fish restaurant dating back to the 1930s on a small square opposite the Scheldt tunnel entrance. The interior is decorated with wood panelling and nostalgic photographs of the port, while a fire blazes in the winter. Locals come here to eat the freshest Ostend sole, Zeeland mussels, oysters and eel.

15 DE ZEESTER

Wandeldijk 28
Left Bank ⑪
+32 (0)3 219 02 06
www.dezeester.be

Antwerp locals have been crossing the river to the St Anna beach since the 1930s to sit on the sand and watch the ships sail past. The beach is not so appealing now, but people still like to come to De Zeester to eat mussels and frites in a traditional Belgian setting, warmed by a blazing fire in winter. It's just a 20-minute walk from town, but feels like somewhere on the North Sea.

The 5 best restaurants to
EAT LIKE A LOCAL

---

16 ARME DUIVEL
Arme Duivelstraat 1
Central Antwerp ①
+32 (0)3 232 26 98

People come here for reliable Belgian cooking served in a reassuringly old interior. The steaks and stews are very good, but the real attraction for many is the chance to eat a horsemeat steak (something of a Belgian speciality). It's a small restaurant, so it is worth booking ahead.

17 DEN ARTIST
Museumstraat 45
Het Zuid ②
+32 (0)3 238 09 95
www.brasseriedenartist.be

This is a serious brasserie decorated with red banquettes and old photographs. The waiters wear long aprons to add to the sense that you are dining out in Paris. But the menu is resolutely Belgian, with hearty specialities such as Flemish *stoofvlees* (stew).

18 CHEZ FRED
Kloosterstraat 83
Central Antwerp ①
+ 32 (0)3 257 14 71
www.chezfred.be

This lively café-restaurant is located amid the antique shops on Kloosterstraat. It is popular with everyone around, from cool fashion designers to noisy family groups. It offers excellent *garnaalkroketjes* (shrimp croquettes), generous steaks and sustaining *stoofvlees* (stew). The Durex sign above the entrance is puzzling.

19 VARKENSPOOT

Graanmarkt 3
Central Antwerp ①
+32 (0)3 232 63 63

Situated on a quiet square behind the Bourla theatre, this is a relaxed Antwerp institution offering wholesome Belgian food. As well as the inevitable *varkenspoten* (pig's trotters served as a starter), the menu features a hearty pea soup in winter, asparagus in spring and rabbit simmered in Hoegaarden beer in autumn.

20 DE KLEINE ZAVEL

Stoofstraat 2
Central Antwerp ①
+32 (0)3 231 96 91
www.kleinezavel.be

Down a lane near the river, De Kleine Zavel is a traditional bistro furnished with wood floors, an old dresser and stacks of wooden beer crates. It has attracted a long list of celebrity clients including international fashion designers and rock stars. They come for the old Antwerp atmosphere as well as the creative cooking.

18 **CHEZ FRED**

The 5 most
STYLISH RESTAURANTS

---

21 **DE MARKT**
Felix Pakhuis
Godefriduskaai 30
Het Eilandje ⑧
+32 (0)3 203 03 30
www.demarkt.nu

Here is a stunning place to eat on the ground floor of the huge St Felix warehouse. The old industrial interior with its impressive rows of cast iron columns has been restored, the walls whitewashed and bare light bulbs hung from the ceiling. Children can pass the time playing in a bright blue caravan parked in a corner. Perfect for a simple lunch after visiting the MAS.

22 **HUNGRY HENRIETTA**
Lombardenvest 19
Central Antwerp ①
+ 32 (0)3 232 29 28
www.hungryhenrietta.be

Named after an American comic book character, Hungry Henrietta has been around since 1973, but moved to its current location on the edge of the fashion district in 1999. Everything here is black – the walls, the Eames chairs and even the staff uniforms. The interior might suggest minimalism, but the kitchen turns out honest Belgian food made with the best ingredients. We recommend the North Sea sole served with grey shrimps and sour cream.

23 L'EPICERIE DU CIRQUE

Volkstraat 23
Het Zuid ②
+32 (0)3 238 05 71
www.lepicerieducirque.be

After working seven years at the Kleine Zavel, Chef Dennis Broeckx and his wife Ellen De Stuyver decided that they knew enough about the trade to open their own restaurant in a former grocery store. Behind the Art Nouveau façade, they have created a relaxed restaurant with a modern Scandinavian interior.

24 LE ZOUTE ZOEN

Zirkstraat 23
Central Antwerp ①
+32 (0)3 226 92 20
www.lezoutezoen.be

Le Zoute Zoen (The Salty Kiss) is a beautiful restaurant on a quiet street that was once in the red light district. The interior is decorated with thick white tablecloths, gilded mirrors and bookshelves along one wall. Viviane Verheyen, considered one of the country's best women chefs, offers an imaginative menu with elements of Belgian, French and Italian cooking. The perfect place for a romantic meal.

25 DE VERANDA

Guldenvliesstraat 60
Zurenborg ⑥
+32 (0)3 218 55 95

Located in a former pharmacist's shop in a district of flamboyant 19th century architecture, De Veranda has kept its old interior. So you are surrounded by dark wood-panelled walls and a large photograph of two sad girls. Davy Schelleman is the chef and his cooking is exceptional. You have no chance of eating here if you do not book many days ahead.

The 5 best restaurants with
GARDENS *and* TERRACES

---

26 **HIPPODROOM**
Leopold de Waelplaats 10
Het Zuid ②
+32 (0)3 248 52 52
www.hippodroom.be

The hippodrome was demolished a long time ago, but this cool modern restaurant has kept the name alive. It opened in 1999 in an old town house renovated by the Antwerp architect Jan Meersman. It is a stunning contemporary brasserie with wood floors, marble tables and neon lights. The cooking is as imaginative as the décor and the back garden is the perfect spot to sit out under the stars in the summer.

27 **ZUIDERTERRAS**
Ernest van Dijckkaai 37
Central Antwerp ①
+32 (0)3 234 12 75
www.zuiderterras.be

The Antwerp architect Bob van Reeth designed this handsome waterfront restaurant which looks like a white ocean liner moored on the Scheldt waterfront. People love the porthole windows and modernist toilets, along with the sweeping river views. The menu includes generous salads, shrimp croquettes and steamed cod with gratinated lemon sabayon.

28 DANIELI IL DIVINO

28 DANIELI IL DIVINO

Beukenlaan 12
Suburbs (Middelheim) ⑫
+32 (0)3 825 37 38
www.danieli-il-divino.be

This beautiful restaurant occupies a rustic building that was once a coach house belonging to Den Brandt castle. The interior is deeply romantic, while a large conservatory at the back provides a gorgeous spot for summer dining. The kitchen produces classic Italian cooking along with the occasional special dish chalked up on the blackboard.

29 GRAND CAFÉ LEROY

Kasteelpleinstraat 49
Central Antwerp ①
+32 (0)3 226 11 99
www.grandcafeleroy.be

Located in a handsome 19th century town house, this is the perfect urban restaurant for outdoor eating on a long summer evening. You pass through the old coach gate to enter the garden, which has wooden decking and plants in big pots. The chef creates some interesting and unusual dishes that are full of flavour.

30 CAMPING CAMPINA

Dageraadplaats 16
Zurenborg ⑥
+32 (0)3 289 54 50

This friendly neighbourhood bistro overlooks the lively open space of Dageraadplaats. The kitchen serves typical Belgian food, along with generous salads and pasta dishes. The cooking is plain, but people come here for the atmosphere, especially on summer nights when the tables are set out under the old trees and the square is lit by a magical canopy of tiny lights

The 5 best

ITALIAN RESTAURANTS

31 **I FAMOSI**
Steenbergstraat 11
Central Antwerp ①
+32 (0)3 231 29 01
www.ifamosi.be

This noisy restaurant near the Nationalestraat is a favourite with fashion designers and models. The walls are covered with photographs of seductive Italian film stars like Sophia Loren and Monica Belucci. The atmosphere is convivial, although the tables are rather close together.

32 **FERRIER 30**
Leopold de Waelplaats 30
Het Zuid ②
+32 (0)3 216 50 62
www.ferrier-30.be

Located near Ann Demeulemeester's shop in Het Zuid, this stylish restaurant has a severe black and white interior. Designed in 2004 by the architect Sofie Pittoors, it offers Italian cooking made with the finest ingredients. A favourite spot to dine in the neighbourhood.

33 **IL GALLO NERO**
Grote Pieter Potstraat 36
Central Antwerp ①
+32 (0)3 231 19 60

This small, convivial restaurant is hidden down a cobbled lane near Grote Markt. It is run with flair by Bruno Trapani from Abruzzo and his Flemish wife Ann Pieters. The couple offer their customers authentic regional cooking from Italy in an intimate setting.

34 **LA NOSTRA CASA**

Dageraadplaats 21
Zurenborg ⑥
+32 (0)3 236 74 52

This small restaurant is the perfect place to enjoy simple Italian cooking. It is decorated with wood floors, pale wood tables and low lighting to create a relaxed ambience. The pizza La Nostra Casa is made the Italian way with a crisp base. You can accompany it with a carafe of good house wine and end with a perfect espresso.

35 **ARTE**

Suikerrui 24
Central Antwerp ①
+32 (0)3 226 29 70
www.ristorante-arte.be

A hip Italian restaurant with white walls, linen table cloths and purple neon lights. The chefs can be seen at work in the kitchen cooking traditional Italian pizzas and pastas. A bit more sophisticated than most Italian restaurants, and a bit more expensive.

The 5 best places to eat in
CHINATOWN

---

36 ORIENTAL DELIGHT
Van Wesenbekestraat 46
Station Quarter ④
+32 (0)3 232 15 83
www.orientaldelight.be

This is an authentic Chinese restaurant with mirrors, dragons and big round tables designed for family meals. The cooking happens out of sight in a huge kitchen where chefs prepare delicious dim sum specialities and large steaming dishes of pork or prawns. The staff are friendly and everyone seems to have fun.

37 FONG MEI
Van Arteveldestraat 65
Station Quarter ④
+32 (0)3 225 06 54
www.fong-mei.weebly.com

This Chinese restaurant does not look too promising. It has rather old furniture, stacks of wine boxes lying around and a single photograph of Hong Kong at night for decoration. But don't be put off. This is one of the best Chinese restaurants in the country, especially if you are on the hunt for authentic dim sum. The chef learned his craft in Hong Kong and prepares each dish with exceptional care. Some wonderful sensations are produced (try number 12). And the people who work here are charming.

38 D.K.
Van Wesenbekestraat 44
Station Quarter ④
+32 (0)3 233 25 78

This modest Chinese restaurant looks old-fashioned, but the food is outstanding. The chef works in a little brick cabin at the front, creating delicious authentic dishes like Singapore-style fried rice noodles and beef tripe with ginger. The waitress greets you with a friendly smile and warns about spicy dishes.

39 THE BEST
Van Wesenbekestraat 57
Station Quarter ④
+32 (0)3 295 75 25
www.restaurantthebest.be

The interior is plain, like most Chinese restaurants, but the food is perfectly cooked and served in generous portions. You can have a quick lunch here or book a large round table for a special meal.

40 LUNG WAH
Van Wesenbekestraat 38
Station Quarter ④
+32 (0)3 297 82 5

The place is a mess, with piles of paperwork, unwashed dishes, stacks of *Euro Dragon News* (the local Chinese newspaper). You squeeze past the kitchen to get into the dining room. A television is tuned to a Chinese reality show. You might think that this is a place to avoid. But exceptional things happen in the kitchen. You should try the crispy Peking duck, or the pork with fried noodles. You soon forget the mess.

The 5 best places for
BURGERS and
BEEFSTEAKS

---

41 DE VEEHANDEL

Lange Lobroekstraat 61
Antwerpen-Noord ⑨
+32 (0)3 271 06 06
www.de-veehandel.be

Located in an old meat hall opposite the slaughterhouse, this is a traditional Belgian restaurant with wood panelling, mirrors and white tablecloths. As the name suggests, De Veehandel (The Cattle Trade) specialises in huge steaks made with the very best Limousin beef. Not a place for vegetarians.

42 DEN ABATTOIR

Lange Lobroekstraat 65
Antwerpen-Noord ⑨
+32 (0)3 271 08 71
www.denabattoir.be

The name tells you everything you need to know. Den Abattoir is a serious meat restaurant located opposite the slaughterhouse, where business deals are struck over a large steak or sausage with *stoemp* (mashed potato and carrots). You can often eat a summer lunch on the terrace.

43 AU VIEUX PORT

Napelsstraat 130
Het Eilandje ⑧
+32 (0)3 290 77 11

Here is a dockside restaurant that serves old Belgian classics like steak and frites, tomatoes with shrimps and *steak tartare* (raw mince). The owner Jan Bogaerts bought the façade in Lille and furnished the interior with old French tables and chairs. The tiled floor and wood panelling add to the atmosphere.

44 WATTMAN

Tramplein 3
Zurenborg ⑥
+32 (0)3 230 55 40
www.wattman.be

Here is the perfect place for lunch after a walk through the flamboyant Zurenborg district. The café, which overlooks a tram depot, takes its name from the 'Wattmen' who drove the old electric trams. The interior is relaxed, with cushions for lounging. The list of burgers is limited to Wattburger, Double Wattburger and Veggie Wattburger. The terrace is the perfect spot to watch the old trams go past.

45 BURGERIJ

Sint Laureiskaai 8
Het Eilandje ⑧
+32 (0)3 336 66 63
www.burgerij.be

This is an excellent burger restaurant just a few minutes from the MAS museum. It occupies a vast industrial space furnished with tables made from recycled wood. The burgers are made with top quality Blanc Bleu Belge beef and served with a tasty barbeque sauce, crisp salad and impeccable frites. The area behind the curtain has a play room filled with toys. The sister restaurant in the Zurenborg district (Tramplein) follows the same basic concept.

The 5 most original
ASIAN RESTAURANTS

46 **UMAMI**
Luikstraat 6
Het Zuid ②
+32 (0)3 237 39 78
www.umami-antwerp.be

This vast Asian restaurant opened in 2012 in a renovated 19th century docklands warehouse. It is a smart, noisy place that feels like New York or London. The cooking is contemporary Asian style which means that the chefs are familiar with the traditions of Japan, China and Thailand.

47 **YAM THAI**
Volkstraat 76
Het Zuid ②
+32 (0)471 82 42 75
www.yamthai.be

The interior is bright and contemporary while the pavement terrace overlooks the Royal Fine Arts Museum. The Thai chef attracts a young fashionable crowd with traditional dishes like Pad Thai.

48 **BIJ LAM & YIN**
Reyndersstraat 17
Central Antwerp ①
+32 (0)3 232 88 38
www.lam-en-yin.be

It is easy to miss this discreet Chinese restaurant located in an old brick town house dating back to 1594. Yet this is probably the best Cantonese restaurant in town. Yin-Yin Pang provide a warm welcome when you arrive while Lap Yee Lam cooks authentic dishes including a delicious crispy duck. Worth booking a table as it is only open five evenings a week.

49 AZUMA

Verlatstraat 39
Het Zuid ②
+32 (0)3 288 58 99
www.azuma-asiandining.be

Hidden down a side street near Ann Demeulemeester's shop, this restaurant is decorated with black wood furniture, white walls and bare light bulbs. All very zen. The chefs work in an open kitchen at the back with sizzling pans and gleaming knives. The menu, as you would expect, has miso soup, sushi mix and sashimi mix, but also Indonesian dishes like babi pangang. Lunch is exceptional value.

50 CUICHINE

Draakstraat 13
Zurenborg ⑥
+32 (0)3 289 92 45
www.cuichine.be

A modern Chinese restaurant with an open kitchen at the back where you can watch the talented chefs at work. The cooking is fresh and sophisticated while the prices remain reasonable. Try the dim sum followed by Peking duck. On summer nights, you can sit in a walled courtyard under the stars.

46 UMAMI

The 5 best
JAPANESE
RESTAURANTS

---

51 **KO'UZI**
Sint-Jorispoort 22
Central Antwerp ①
+32 (0)3 232 24 88
www.kouzi.be

Junko Kawada is an outstanding sushi chef who prepares individual sushi portions as well as artistic lunch kits that include soup, fresh fish and chopped vegetables. Kawada has adapted to Belgium by incorporating local ingredients such as grey North Sea shrimps and even chocolate.

52 **ROJI**
Oude Koornmarkt 26
Central Antwerp ①
+32 (0)3 296 61 33
www.roji.be

Here is the most secret sushi restaurant in Antwerp. A small sign is all you can see from the street. You have to descend a flight of steps to reach the vaulted cloister of a 13th-century monastery. The sushi is delicious, although the food is sometimes slow to arrive.

53 **YAMAYA SANTATSU**
Ossenmarkt 19
University Quarter ③
+32 (0)3 234 09 49
www.santatsu.be

Here is an authentic Japanese restaurant on a quiet square in the university quarter. Founded in 1988, it is a favourite with Japanese executives based in Antwerp. They come because everything is correct, from the hospitable atmosphere to the delicate portions of sushi made with the freshest fish.

54 IZUMI

Beeldhouwersstraat 44
Het Zuid ②
+32 (0)3 216 13 79
www.izumi.be

This authentic Japanese restaurant was founded in 1978 in a white town house in Het Zuid. The owner is Dutch, but spent two years in Japan learning about the cooking traditions. On his return to the Low Countries, he created a typical Japanese interior with seats around the kitchen and sliding wood screens. Then he found a chef who could prepare the perfect sushi.

55 FUJI-SAN

Waalse Kaai 36
Het Zuid ②
+32 (0)3 216 27 53

It's easy to miss this little place in the old warehouse district of Het Zuid. It looks more like a snack bar, but the chef knows his stuff. People cram inside and perch where they can to sample delicious portions of sushi and sashimi. But there is no reason to linger.

51 KOUZI

The 5 best
SANDWICH BARS

---

56 BROOD OP DE PLANK

Lange Kievitstraat 114
Station Quarter ④
+32 (0)472 50 27 73
www.broodopdeplank.be

This sandwich shop near Central Station makes exceptional sandwiches. You can order *Ciabatta toba* (ciabatta bread with parma ham, tomato, mozzarella and green pesto), or *Noordzeeboke* (a brown roll with lettuce, potato salad, tomato, cucumber and North Sea shrimps). This place is very popular with office workers, so the lunchtime queue can be long. Closed at the weekend.

57 CAFFÈ INTERNAZIONALE

Volkstraat 21
Het Zuid ②
+32 (0)3 248 25 00
www.caffeinternazionale.be

Marco Migliore's espresso bar is furnished with a retro mix of metal chairs, tiny round tables and vintage table lamps. The back room even has sofas and a cuckoo clock. Here is the place to come for the best pastrami sandwich in Antwerp – made from seasoned smoked beef, served with pickle, sauerkraut and mustard. The menu also features a sandwich called Heart Attack which contains pastrami, bacon, cheese and an entirely unnecessary fried egg. Cakes are supplied by Les Tartes de Françoise.

58 CÉLESTE

Hoogstraat 77
Central Antwerp ①
+32 (0)473 90 06 97
www.celeste-antwerp.be

Céleste and her husband Ezra run a busy little sandwich bar with checked table cloths, flowers in vases and pots of herbs. The sandwiches are made with traditional French baguettes and the freshest of ingredients. The more healthy sandwiches have names like Detox, Bikini and Body & Soul. Or you can gorge on a generous hamburger.

59 DEN BOTERHAM

Plantinkaai 14
Central Antwerp ①
+32 (0)486 83 87 14

A rustic café-bakery on the Scheldt quays where you can pick up tasty sandwiches made with fresh Italian ciabatta bread. They often have unusual choices on the menu like goat's cheese with apple, bacon and sweet Liège syrup, or chicken with courgette, red onion, mushrooms, warm curry and Parmesan cheese. It's also good for a lazy Sunday breakfast.

60 A TAVOLA

Lange Lozanastraat 282
Southern Antwerp ⑦
+32 (0)3 238 07 09

You are unlikely to stumble upon this little Italian sandwich shop, located in a quiet neighbourhood where tourists have no reason to visit. But it is worth tracking it down if you want a delicious sandwich made with ciabatta bread and wrapped in a cheerful red-and-white checked napkin. You choose the ingredients yourself from a display cabinet filled with tasty Italian hams, sun-dried tomatoes and grilled aubergines.

The 5 best
BRASSERIES

---

61 **CIRO'S**
Amerikalei 6
Het Zuid ②
+32 (0)3 238 11 47
www.ciros.be

Here is a classic Belgian restaurant dating from 1962. The wood-panelled interior has hardly changed since then and the menu still lists old Belgian favourites. So this is where to come if you want a good Irish rib steak served with pepper sauce and a generous portion of frites.

62 **ZURICH**
Verlatstraat 2
Het Zuid ②
+32 (0)3 238 49 67
www.cafezurich.be

This is a bright, bustling bistro with a black-and-white tiled floor, huge mirrors and marble table tops. The young people who work here are exceptionally friendly and fast, while the dish of the day is exceptional value. The bread is served in a silver dish and the frites are perfectly done. We love this place.

63 **ENTREPOT DU CONGO**
Vlaamse Kaai 42
Het Zuid ②
+32 (0)475 528 215
www.entrepotducongo.com

The interior of this brasserie was designed to evoke the mood of an old Antwerp restaurant, so there are mirrors, wood panelling and a photograph of King Baudouin above the bar. A quiet place for coffee in the morning or afternoon, it gets crowded at lunchtime.

64 BOURLA

Graanmarkt 7
Central Antwerp ①
+32 (0)3 223 16 32
www.bourla.be

This beautiful old-style brasserie occupies a former office building near the Bourla theatre. The nostalgic interior is decorated with chandeliers and palm trees, along with vast mirrors and a grand piano. The kitchen produces good Belgian food like shrimp croquettes, Flemish stew and a sole meunière that comes with perfect frites and a pot of homemade mayonnaise.

65 DANSING CHOCOLA

Kloosterstraat 159
Central Antwerp ①
+32 (0)3 237 19 05
www.dansingchocola.be

The old posters, painted ceiling and draped velvet curtains create a theatrical mood. The cooking is plain, but authentic, with something for every type of hunger, from a simple ham sandwich served with a pot of mustard to guinea fowl with port sauce and rösti. We like to sit at a table on the mezzanine sharing a big 75cl bottle of La Chouffe.

61 CIRO'S

The 5 best places for
CHEAP EATS

66 **MADEMOISELLE MOUSTACHE**
Paardenmarkt 21
University Quarter ③
+32 (0)479 81 61 00
www.mademoiselle-moustache.be

You wouldn't expect to find a cool place to eat among the machine tool shops and old bars of the seamen's quarter. But Mademoiselle Moustache has introduced hip vintage design and creative cooking to the neighbourhood. The interior is furnished with odd lamps, quirky postcards pinned to a noticeboard and an old motorbike. The young women who work here are extremely friendly, even when it gets hectic. Good for sandwiches, soups and chocolate cake.

67 **COMME SOUPE**
Hendrik Conscience-plein 11
Central Antwerp ①
+32 (0)3 234 35 33
www.commesoupe.be

In her bright little restaurant near the Carolus Borromeus church, Charlotte Van Hoeck keeps four different homemade soups simmering away in large black pots. She serves the soup in large white bowls along with thick slices of brown bread. This is a friendly and comforting place on a rainy day. We like to escape to the little tables upstairs.

68   DE TALOORKES

Lange Koepoortstraat 61
Central Antwerp ①
+32 (0)3 234 39 98
www.taloorkes.be

This convivial restaurant cooks traditional Flemish dishes such as *stoemp* (mashed potato with carrots) and steak served with chunky homemade frites. You may have to ask about some of the dishes if you don't speak Dutch. Even then, you might wonder what on earth they can mean by *blinde vinken* ('blind finches'). The prices are really low, making De Taloorkes a popular place for students. It can get crowded, but that just adds to the charm.

69   PERRUCHE

Oudevaartplaats 60
Central Antwerp ①
+32 (0)488 25 02 64

Run by a mother and daughter, this café was once a shop selling budgies. The birds have gone, but the interior has been left largely untouched. It is furnished with vintage stools, salvaged doors and potted plants to create a relaxed domestic feel. Mamma works in the kitchen making homemade soup and delicious ciabatta bread sandwiches while her daughter serves and chats to the customers. A good place to head if you are looking for a café terrace on a sunny day.

70   FAIR FOOD

Steenhouwersvest 29
Central Antwerp ①
+32 (0)3 234 97 00
www.fair-food.be

A relaxed restaurant with assorted vintage furniture, pink carnations in vases and quiet jazz playing in the background. The little kitchen produces good organic food including generous bowls of soup, wholesome sandwiches and imaginative salads.

66 MADEMOISELLE MOUSTACHE

MUFFINS MET
CHOCOLA EN
BANAAN

73 IN DE ROSCAM

The 5 best places for a
HEALTHY LUNCH

---

71 **WAANZEE**
Sint Aldegondiskaai 52
Het Eilandje ⑧
+32 (0)3 226 35 87
www.waanzee.be

Located on the waterfront facing MAS, this friendly family-owned café is the perfect place for lunch. The interior is decorated with a beautiful tiled floor, an ancient wooden counter and faded photographs of the port. The woman chef in the kitchen produces delicious sandwiches using thick homemade brown bread served with crisp, fresh vegetables.

72 **LOMBARDIA**
Lombardenvest 78
Central Antwerp ①
+32 (0)3 233 68 19
www.lombardia.be

Located in the heart of the fashion district, Lombardia looks a bit scruffy. It is furnished with an assortment of old round tables and chairs, while the walls are plastered with posters, adverts and newspaper cuttings. You could be forgiven for walking straight past. But this restaurant is an Antwerp institution. It has been serving wholesome vegetarian dishes since 1972. Sting has eaten here. So has the band Sigur Rós. The terrace under the trees is just perfect for a summer lunch.

73 IN DE ROSCAM

Vrijdagmarkt 12
Central Antwerp ①
+32 (0)486 42 56 06

This café on the corner of the Vrijdagmarkt attracts students from the nearby fashion academy. Yet it is homely rather than hip, furnished with an old stove, vintage table lamps and a few dusty books. The women behind the counter know how to cook the perfect comfort food. A bowl of soup served with a thick slice of bread is perfect on a cold winter day.

74 FARINE'S PARIS TEXAS

Vlaamse Kaai 40
Het Zuid ②
+32 (0)499 75 16 17

Farine's is a friendly café on the old docks with an open kitchen and an odd collection of ornaments. It is run by Justine Vanthilt, an American, who serves good food throughout the day. This is a good place for a sustaining breakfast or a healthy bowl of soup at lunchtime, or just to sit outside on the wooden deck with a cold glass of Vedett Blonde.

75 PITTEN & BONEN

Lombardenvest 31
Central Antwerp ①
+32 (0)3 213 28 88
www.pittenenbonen.be

This bright modern café in the heart of the fashion district is decorated with pale wood tables and a big blackboard where the day's menu is written out. The crates of tropical fruit at the door are a sign that this place is determined to serve fresh food. You can order a big bowl of salad or a sandwich made with Italian bread. The fruit juices are superb, but this is slow food, so be prepared for a long wait.

The 5 best places for
PROPER BELGIAN FRITES

---

76 **DE SMULPAEP**
Varkensmarkt 2
University Quarter ③
+32 (0)3 226 26 17

The man behind the counter used to be a French chef before he turned his hand to creating Belgian frites. He is a perfectionist who uses the best vegetable oil. The place is popular with students who like to fill up on comfort food here before a night of drinking.

77 **FLY-INN**
Sint Jacobsstraat 23
University Quarter ③

This is a smart little frites shop in the student quarter with a friendly young woman behind the counter. The potatoes are fried twice until they emerge from the fat looking crisp and golden. They are then brought to your table in a cardboard box.

78 **FRITKOT MAX**
Groenplaats 12
Central Antwerp ①

Fritkot Max sells fluffy Belgian frites in old-fashioned paper cones. You can eat downstairs in a tiny space designed to look like a town square, complete with blue painted ceiling and street lantern, or climb the stairs to a little frites museum decorated with memorabilia collected by a local academic.

79 FRITUUR NUMBER ONE

Hoogstraat 1
Central Antwerp ①

On a winter evening, with the wind blowing off the Schelde, you can fight off the cold with a portion of piping hot frites. The woman behind the counter is called Maria. She likes to tease customers in her thick Antwerp dialect. Someone once placed an order for "a large frites, a mexicano, a currywurst special and … oh, yes, a Diet Coke." Maria promptly replied: "Listen, mate, if you are going to eat all that stuff, you might as well have a normal Coke, eh?"

80 FRITUUR 'T STEEN

Steenplein
Central Antwerp ①

This is a typical aluminium frites shack on the waterfront. You can take your paper cone of frites and sit on a bench watching the ships sail past. Or sit out on the new wooden pier to be even closer to the water.

80 FRITUUR 'T STEEN

The 5 best shops for
FOOD AND WINE

---

81 **CHACALLI**
Geefsstraat 5
Central Antwerp ①
+32 (0)3 609 54 50
www.chacalliwines.com

You enter this shop through a strange vaulted brick room and climb a narrow staircase. It leads into an unexpected 19th century library that once held the bishop's archives. The ancient shelves are filled with remarkable wines. Some bottles are as cheap as €6.

82 **EL VALENCIANO**
Zirkstraat 34
Central Antwerp ①
+32 (0)3 225 01 79
www.elvalenciano.be

Located in a 1505 house called *De Gulde Handt*, this shop opened in the 1950s to serve immigrants who had moved to Antwerp from Franco's Spain. The shop has huge hams hanging from the roof beams, glistening black olives in large tubs and intense wines from the Marqués de Cáceres vineyards.

83 **CRIEE**
Van Wesenbekestraat 21
Station Quarter ④

The aisles down the middle sell standard supermarket products, but the stalls along the side are occupied by specialised food traders. At the Roosemeyers stand, you can buy offal and cold meats, while Bruno Van de Poel sells poultry, and Benny Vermeulen specialises in meat shipped from Paris. Closed Mondays.

84 **SUN WAH SUPERMARKET**
Van Wesenbekestraat 16
Station Quarter ④
+32 (0)3 770 77 14

A large Asian supermarket in the heart of Chinatown with a spectacular assortment of foods that are hard to find anywhere else. They import huge sacks of rice, dozens of varieties of noodles, tinned lychees, green tea and every ingredient you might need for cooking Asian food. The room upstairs sells imported goods like kimonos and little paper lanterns for Chinese festivals.

85 **KAASMEESTER VAN TRICHT**
Fruithoflaan 41
Suburbs (Berchem) ⑫
+32 (0)3 440 14 05
www.kaasmeestervantricht.be

Here is a specialised shop where you find some of the rarest cheeses in Europe. Michel Van Tricht supplies cheese to the Belgian royal family as well as some of the best restaurants in Belgium. He recently added tables to allow customers to sit with a glass of wine and a selection of fine cheeses.

81 CHACALLI

The 5 best
BAKERIES

---

86 **DOMESTIC**
Steenbokstraat 37
Zurenborg ⑥
+32 (0)3 239 98 90
www.domeweb.be

You can smell the baking bread long before you reach this smart white bakery near the railway viaduct. Created by the owners of Dôme on the opposite side of the street, it sells several varieties of bread, along with croissants and lemon tarts.

87 **GOOSSENS**
Korte Gasthuisstraat 31
Central Antwerp ①
+32 (0)3 226 07 91
www.bakkerijgoossens-antwerpen.be

Founded in 1884, this traditional bakery has a beautiful interior with a tiled floor and marble counter. It is famous for its raisin bread, which is piled high in the window. It also makes biscuits and cheesecake. But the shop is small. Four people can just about squeeze inside. Everyone else must wait patiently outside in the rain. Dries van Noten sometimes stops here on his way to the office, but even he has to wait outside.

88 KLEINBLATT

Provinciestraat 206
Station Quarter ④
+32 (0)3 233 75 13
www.kleinblatt.be

Look for the neon sign. That's Kleinblatt's. For more than 100 years, people have been coming to this kosher bakery in the Jewish quarter for sesame seed bread, bagels and cakes. They also make delicious Sachertorte and cheesecake, along with special cakes for Jewish festivals.

89 STEINMETZ

Lange Kievitstraat 64
Station Quarter ④
+32 (0)3 233 67 49

This little kosher bakery near the railway viaduct has been around since 1967. The main reason to come here is for the cheesecake, which is made in large metal trays. You might also want to try the Jewish chocolate and buttercream cookies.

90 LES TARTES DE FRANÇOISE

Ieperstraat 20
Southern Antwerp ⑦
+32 (0)3 216 31 16
www.tartes.be

It looks like a garage. The sign is barely visible. You go through the door and enter an industrial kitchen filled with the smell of baking. Hopefully you have already placed your order online, or you may leave empty handed. Les Tartes de Françoise is a brilliant concept that began in Brussels when a woman called Françoise started baking cakes for her friends. The business has grown larger, but the sweet and savoury tarts are still exceptional.

The 5 best places for
EXOTIC FOOD

---

91 **HOFFY'S**
Lange Kievitstraat 52
Station Quarter ④
+32 (0)3 234 35 35
www.hoffys.be

The Hoffman brothers opened this authentic kosher restaurant just behind Central Station in 1985. They are older now, but the food is just the same. This is where Orthodox Jews come to pick up takeaway food from the counter at the entrance or eat in the restaurant at the back. It's a serious, rather formal place, and it isn't cheap. But the food is outstanding.

92 **O'TAGINE**
Leopold de Waelstraat 20
Het Zuid ②
+32 (0)3 237 06 19

Here is an idyllic Moroccan restaurant in Het Zuid where you can eat couscous, tagines or bowls of traditional Moroccan soup. The interior is romantically lit with candles and decorated with tiles, cushions and painted wood doors. We recommend the Tagine Kasbah made with plums and grilled almonds. For summer eating, there is a small terrace on the street and an intimate garden at the back.

93 BENI FALAFEL

Lange Leemstraat 188
Jewish Quarter ⑤
+32 (0)3 218 82 11

Located in the heart of Jewish Antwerp, this looks like a simple snack bar. But Beni, the owner, serves the best falafel in town. He bakes flat bread on an iron plate and fills the inside with hummus and sauerkraut. The place is packed with school students and diamond workers at lunchtimes, but less frantic in the evening.

94 SAFFRAAN

Geuzenstraat 15
Het Zuid ②
+32 (0)3 237 66 56
www.resto-saffraan.be

Mashuk Rahaman opened this attractive Indian restaurant in 2003. The interior is decorated with two impressive carved wooden doors, while the walls are painted a soft yellow. The cooking is based on different Indian regional traditions, with tandoori dishes made in an authentic oven brought over from London and nan bread freshly baked every day.

95 EL WARDA

Draakstraat 4
Zurenborg ⑥
+32 (0)3 239 31 13
www.elwarda.be

A stunning North African restaurant in Zurenborg decorated with cushions and candles. The Tunisian chef, Fatima Marzouki, who has written several cookbooks, makes delicious North African appetisers served in little bowls and delicately-flavoured tagines using chicken and honey or prunes.

The 5 best places for
SUNDAY BRUNCH

96 JAM
Wolstraat 47
Central Antwerp ①
+ 32 (0)3 233 36 12

This friendly café near the art academy offers a generous breakfast that is served throughout the day. The look is vintage chic, with cracked tiled walls, old school chairs and formica tables. The terrace is a lovely spot when the sun shines, with its random assortment of chairs, sofas and deckchairs.

97 DE BIOLOGISCH-DYNAMISCHE BAKKERIJ
Volkstraat 17
Het Zuid ②
+32 (0)3 216 00 42

Here is a friendly bohemian bakery/café with worn wooden floorboards, rustic furniture and an old iron stove. Founded by the Chilean Carlos Maldonado more than a decade ago, this popular place uses healthy ingredients to make its bread and cakes.

98 DAILY ROAST
Hoogstraat 13
Central Antwerp ①
+32 (0)3 225 24 54

The house where the painter Jacob Jordaens was born is now a coffee shop where the aroma of freshly-roasted coffee beans drifts out into the street. This is a relaxed place to spend a Sunday morning sipping a coffee from Kenya.

99 STORM

Hanzestedenplaats 5
Het Eilandje ⑧
+32 (0)3 231 43 00
www.cafe-storm.com

The MAS museum café is the ideal location for a weekend brunch. The interior designer Kurt Hereygers of Not Before Ten created the austere industrial look using plain metal lamps, black tables and a wall of quirky shelves. It also has a terrace with benches that catch the morning sun. The brunch menu will set you up for a brisk walk through the old port area.

100 HET DAGELIJKS BROOD

Lange Kievitstraat 107
Station Quarter ④
+32 (0)3 226 37 10
www.lepainquotidien.be

The Brussels café-bakery chain Le Pain Quotidien (known as Het Dagelijks Brood in Flanders) recently opened a third branch in Antwerp at the back of Centraal Station. The interior is a familiar mix of rustic furniture, racks of round bread and sticky pots of jam. But the location is very modern. You can sit with your bowl of coffee watching trains glide into the sleek new station and then set off on a walk around the Jewish district.

99 STORM

103 MOMADE CUPCAKES

The 5 best places for
DELICIOUS CAKES

---

101 **HET GEBAAR**

Leopoldstraat 24
Central Antwerp ①
+32 (0)3 232 37 10
www.hetgebaar.be

Here is a seriously romantic place for lunch, in a rustic 19th century building in a corner of the botanical gardens where the head gardener once lived. Chef Roger van Damme now occupies the building, cooking inventive lunch dishes using the best ingredients. His desserts are stunning.

102 **STARFISH & COFFEE**

Bresstraat 9
Southern Antwerp ⑦
+32 (0)486 98 79 77
*Starfishandcoffeeantwerpen.
blogspot.be*

Katja Matthyns has created cake heaven on the south side of town. Her friendly, cluttered café is decorated with bare wood floors, worn armchairs and old family photos. As well as baking her own bread, Katja makes muffins, applecake and tasty biscuits with lots of seeds and cereals (called Twiet Twiet). Her chocolate cake vanishes almost as soon as it comes out of the oven.

103 MOMADE CUPCAKES

Reynderstraat 37
Central Antwerp ①
+32 (0)3 233 33 23
www.momadecupcakes.be

Mo Lamkoref opened a tiny shop near the cathedral in 2011 where he sells more than 30 varieties of cupcakes. He gets up before dawn to work on his creations, which incorporate exotic hints of lavender, ginger and speculoos biscuit. Mo also serves perfect Illy coffee in a tiny space that seats barely six people.

104 LOJOLA

Hendrik Conscience-
plein 14
Central Antwerp ①
+32 (0)3 293 63 86

Jolien Van der Stighelen runs a tiny coffee bar just off the beautiful Hendrik Conscienceplein. Young women from the neighbourhood come here to chat or update their fashion blog while nibbling on bright pink cupcakes. With its old sofas and baking smells, this place feels more like grandmother's front room than an urban hotspot. When the weather allows, a few deck chairs are put out into the square.

105 'T SUUT BEKSKE

Hoogstraat 54
Central Antwerp ①
+32 (0)3 232 22 60

There is barely room to move in this tiny tea room furnished with old wooden tables, Art Nouveau lamps and shelves lined with antique coffee grinders. But you can sometimes find a table upstairs. This friendly place serves six different types of breakfast from 9 am as well as lunch and afternoon tea.

The 5 best shops for
BELGIAN CHOCOLATES

---

106 GOOSSENS CHOCOLATIER

Isabellalei 6
Jewish Quarter ⑤
+32 (0)3 239 13 10
www.goossens-chocolatier.com

Not too easy to find, Goossens is a small chocolate shop in the Jewish quarter where Erik Goossens makes chocolates by hand in a back room. Some years ago, the US ambassador set out to find the best chocolate shop in Belgium and found himself in Goossens' little shop. They were the best, he decided, which landed Mr Goossens with a contract to supply chocolates to the White House every year.

107 DOMINIQUE PERSOONE

Paleis op de Meir
Wapper 2
Central Antwerp ①
+32 (0)3 206 20 30
www.dominiquepersoone.be

Dominique Persoone is the enfant terrible of Belgian chocolate makers. When he opened his first shop in Bruges, people could scarcely believe that he used flavours like smoked eel, fried bacon and cauliflower. But then he was awarded a place in the Michelin guide and people became less wary. His latest venture in Antwerp is located in two rooms of the former royal palace once occupied by Napoleon's brother.

108 BURIE

Korte Gasthuisstraat 3
Central Antwerp ①
+32 (0)3 232 36 88
www.chocolatier-burie.be

Hans Burie opened a little chocolate shop in Antwerp in 1969. His son now runs the place, creating delicious home-made chocolates using cocoa beans imported from Ghana and the Ivory Coast. He also creates beautiful chocolate sculptures which are displayed in the window.

109 DEL REY

Appelmansstraat 5
Station Quarter ④
+32 (0)3 470 28 61
www.delrey.be

Hidden down a side street in the diamond district, Del Rey has been selling handmade chocolates since 1949. With its stark modern interior, it could almost be another diamond shop. As well as redesigning the shop, the owners have introduced various novelties, including a bar where they serve 12 different types of chocolate milk, a new line in macaroons and chocolates in the shape of diamonds.

110 GÜNTHER WATTÉ

Steenhouwersvest 30
Central Antwerp ①
+32 (0)3 293 58 94
www.watte.be

Günther Watté sells chocolates in a beautiful baroque interior that looks more like an expensive jeweller's shop. He also serves coffee in the lounge at the back along with a chocolate and a glass of amaretto. You can watch the chocolate makers at work in the back room through a glass wall.

107 DOMINIQUE PERSOONE

111 BROUWERIJ DE KONINCK

The 5 specialities to
EAT AND DRINK
before you leave

---

111 DE KONINCK

BREWERY AT:
Mechelsesteenweg 291
Southern Antwerp ⑦
www.dekoninck.com

Antwerp's distinctive dark ale is brewed in an old whitewashed brewery on the road to Mechelen. It dates back to 1833 when the De Koninck family opened a brewery called *De Hand* in a country inn. In 2010 the brewery was sold to the Duvel Moortgat group, but the beer is still served in a distinctive bolleke glass.

112 ANTWERPSE HANDJES

FOUND AT:
Philip's Biscuits
Korte Gasthuisstraat 39
Central Antwerp ①
+32 (0)3 231 26 60
www.philipsbiscuits.be

This buttery biscuit was invented in 1934 by local baker and won a competition organised by the Association of Master Bakers to create a new culinary delicacy for the city. It takes its name (and its shape) from the Antwerp legend of the hand thrown into the River Scheldt. You may get one served with your coffee in a local café. Otherwise you can find them in traditional baker's shops such as Philip's Biscuits.

113 ELIXIR D'ANVERS

BREWERY AT:
Haantjeslei 132
Southern Antwerp ⑦
www.elixir-danvers.be

François-Xavier de Beukelaer invented this sweet golden liqueur in Antwerp in 1863. Flavoured with 32 herbs and spices, it is regarded by some as a miracle cure for almost every ailment. But the high alcohol content suggests this legend may be something of a myth.

114 BROODJE MARTINO

FOUND AT:
Van Helmont
Hopland 27
Central Antwerp ①
+32 (0)3 232 56 81

Nobody can exactly agree on the origins of the *broodje Martino*. Some say it was invented in the 1950s in a sandwich shop on Antwerp's De Coninckplein but others argue that it comes from Ghent. It is made with a crisp baguette filled with raw minced beef, cucumber, red onion, anchovies and gherkins. But the most important ingredient is a secret spicy sauce made from various ingredients including Tabasco, ketchup, mustard and a dash of Worcester sauce.

115 SEEF BIER

FOUND AT:
Zeppelin
Damplein 13
Antwerpen-Noord ⑨
+32 (0)3 689 16 62

Here is a beer worth tracking down. It was launched in 2012 by Johan Van Dyck, a local beer enthusiast who wanted to bring back the taste of old Antwerp ales. Based on an ancient recipe found in a shoebox, this cloudy yellow beer comes in a chunky bottle with a retro label. Flavoured with hints of grain and hops, Seef Bier won a gold medal in the Belgian-style ale category at the 2012 World Beer Cup in San Diego.

CAFFÈ INTERNAZIONALE

55 PLACES
FOR A DRINK

The 5 most
BEAUTIFUL CAFES

---

116 LE ROYAL CAFÉ
Koningin Astridplein 27
Station Quarter ④
+32 (0)3 233 12 77

Antwerp has always liked to impress its visitors, as is clear the moment you step off the train at Centraal Station. The vast entrance hall has grand staircases and a magnificent dome, while the station café is decorated with moulded ceilings, high mirrors and an enormous clock.

117 DE FOYER
Komedieplaats 19
Central Antwerp ①
+32 (0)3 233 55 17
www.bourlaschouwburg.be

The grandest café in Antwerp is found on the first floor of the Bourla Theatre. It was designed by the architect Pierre Bourla, with a vaulted ceiling, frescos and mirrors. The coffee is excellent and the tea comes in a porcelain teapot. You can come here for a classic Belgian steak and frites.

118 GUSTAV
Van Ertbornstraat 2
Station Quarter ④
+32 (0)3 225 55 28
www.brasseriegustav.be

The interior looks like an old Vienna coffee house decorated with vaulted ceilings, marble columns and green fake leather benches. There are waiters in black uniforms and napkins embroidered with a G. It is the perfect place to meet a friend for coffee while sad blues music plays in the background.

119 CAFÉ IMPERIAL

Meir 50
Central Antwerp ①
+32 (0)3 206 20 20
www.cafe-imperial.be

One wing of the old royal palace on Meir has been turned into a stylish café with four separate rooms, ranging from grand to intimate. The coffee is served with a home-made chocolate from Dominique Persoone's workshop in the opposite wing of the palace.

120 GRAND CAFÉ DE SINGEL

Jan van Rijswijcklaan 155
Southern Antwerp ⑦
+32 (0)3 237 71 00
www.grandcafedesingel.be

Located in a glass cube designed by Stéphane Beel, this is a striking space with sweeping views. The café occupies a large open space, while the restaurant is in a separate area behind the bar, overlooking a motorway. They subscribe to an impressive selection of newspapers and magazines including *The New York Review of Books*.

120 GRAND CAFÉ DE SINGEL

The 5 best bars to
DRINK WITH
THE LOCALS

---

121 **DE DUIFKENS**
Graanmarkt 5
Central Antwerp ①
+32 (0)3 225 10 39

Here is an absolutely authentic Antwerp brown café. It is a friendly place popular with actors, writers and musicians. Decorated with nostalgic theatre posters and faded photographs of Belgian actors, this is one of the most artistic cafés in town.

122 **DE VISMIJN**
Riemstraat 20
Het Zuid ②
+32 (0)3 238 45 60
www.cafedevismijn.be

This handsome old brown café from 1930 used to serve workers from the nearby fish market, but the people here are now more likely to be antique dealers and property developers. Yet this still has the feel of a local bar with its dark interior and old photographs of Antwerp's docklands. The bar is run by Yves Van Roy who won the Belgian barman of the year award in 2009.

123 **KASSA 4**
Ossenmarkt 21
University Quarter ③
+32 (0)3 227 21 65

Here is a hip bar decorated with old wood and mirrors. Located in the heart of the student quarter, Kassa 4 attracts a lively mix of students, philosophers and musicians.

124 CAFÉ BEVEREN

Vlasmarkt 2
Central Antwerp ①
+32 (0)495 81 81 34

This is an authentic port bar with the only Decap organ to survive in Antwerp. You can hear the flamboyant 1930s Art Deco dance organ belting out some nostalgic melody long before you reach the door.

125 DE KONINCKLIJKE SNOR

Adriaan Brouwerstraat 33
Het Eilandje ⑧
+32 (0)3 226 01 98

The Antwerp moustache club meets in a café called De Konincklijke Snor (The Royal Moustache), decorated with photographs of former winners of the Moustache of the Year Award (among them a former mayor and a walrus in Antwerp zoo). but the strangest mementoes are connected to the annual trip to the Independent Republic of Snoravia, a small island in the River Maas colonised by the moustache club members.

122 DE VAGISMIJN

The 5 most
STYLISH CAFES

---

126 VITRIN
Marnixplaats 14
Het Zuid ②
+32 (0)48 517 9858
www.vitrin.eu

The plywood walls and the long benches of this bright café and cocktail bar were designed by the friendly young owners Michiel Thys and Kenny Aernouts. The pavement terrace faces west so you can sit outside in the evening with a glass of their signature spritz (cava, aperol and a slice of orange) as the sun sets. We love this place.

127 LA CHASCONA
Oever 18
Central Antwerp ①

Here is a cool café that serves the perfect espresso coffee in a little china cup. The interior is decorated with worn sofas picked up at the Vrijdagmarkt, piles of fashion magazines and a bright pink flamingo. Most of the furniture here is for sale.

128 KORSAKOV
Sint-Jorispoort 1
Central Antwerp ①
+32 (0)485 46 45 06

Korsakov's interior is pure 1950s, with a tiled floor and red formica tables tops. The metal spiral staircase leads to a romantic upper room where smoking is allowed. Some basic food is served.

129 ZEPPELIN

Damplein 13
Antwerpen-Noord ⑨
+32 (0)3 689 16 62

With its crumbling architecture and raw urban feel, Damplein has something of the mood of Berlin. Zeppelin adds to the effect. The two-room interior has bare brick walls with flaking plaster and flea market furniture. The women who run this bar create a relaxed mood where everyone feels at home.

130 HANGAR 41

Sint Michielskaai 41
Het Zuid ②
+32 (0)3 257 09 18
www.hangareenenveertig.be

Located in a corner building close to the Scheldt waterfront, this is a stylish urban café with lofty ceilings, bare wood floors and a pavement terrace. The kitchen offers simple dishes at a reasonable price, making this the perfect place to end a stroll around Antwerp's fashionable south side.

126 VITRIN

The 5 best bars for
JAZZ AND BLUES

---

131 **DE MUZE**
Melkmarkt 15
Central Antwerp ①
+32 (0)3 226 01 26
www.jazzmuze.be

In this moody old jazz bar, many still remember the 1960s when the bearded Ferre Grignard stood on the little stage at the back. Not much has changed: the café is still a dark, rambling place with bare brick walls, roof beams and a warren of alcoves. Live jazz concerts happen most nights at 22.00 or on Sundays at 15.00.

132 **HOPPER**
Leopold de Waelstraat 2
Het Zuid ②
+32 (0)3 248 49 33
www.cafehopper.be

This might look like a plain café, but its regulars include some famous musicians, artists and actors. During the day, this is a relaxed place with jazz playing gently in the background. But it gets noisy in the evening, when musicians come here to perform.

133 **CROSSROADS CAFE**
Paardenmarkt 115
University Quarter ③
+32 (0)3 231 52 66
www.crossroadscafe.be

This friendly brown café on the Paardenmarkt attracts a mix of customers, from retired dock workers to Australian backpackers. Some come here to play pool or the old Flemish game vogelpik. Others head this way on Sundays for the live blues gigs.

134 KIEBOOMS

De Coninckplein 18
Antwerpen-Noord ⑨

Most of the interior of this unique bar was designed in 1949 when the accordionist Leo Kiebooms bought the place and redecorated it with neon lights, formica tables and a tiny stage. Closed for 20 years, it reopened in 2011 as a beautiful jazz venue where crowds pile inside to hear the band Radio Muzak or singer Sofie Dijkmans.

135 ZEEZICHT

Dageraadplaats 7
Zurenborg ⑥
+32 (0)3 235 10 65

A rambling bohemian café decorated with old battered tables, metal pipes and tangled wires. Random philosophical quotes appear on the walls. This might sound like a student dive, but it is popular with everyone from artists to young mothers. Jazz and blues concerts are held most Sunday evenings.

The 5 bars with the
LONGEST BEER LISTS

---

136 'T WAAGSTUK
Stadswaag 20
University Quarter ③
+32 (0)3 225 02 19
www.waagstuk.be

This old bar occupies a former 16th century warehouse. The friendly owners Lucy and Dieter keep seven beers on tap and about 100 different bottled beers, including the dark house ale named Zeppelin. Look out for the monthly beer seminars organised in the back room by the Antwerp Beer College.

137 BIERHUIS KULMINATOR
Vleminckveld 32-34
Central Antwerp ①
+32 (0)3 232 45 38

Beer fans love this place because of its 40-page menu listing 800 or so ales, many of them hard to find anywhere else, like Verdominis Wild Turkey Barrel Aged and Struisse Shark Pants. The café was rated best beer bar in the world in 2012.

138 PATERS VAETJE
Blauwmoezelstraat 1
Central Antwerp ①
+32 (0)3 231 84 76
www.patersvaetje.be

The best feature of this bar is the terrace located right under the Cathedral tower. The interior is tiny and often crowded, but you might find a table on the floor above. The bar has about six beers on tap and a further 70 or so in bottles.

139 DE GROOTE WITTE AREND

Reyndersstraat 18
Central Antwerp ①
+32 (0)3 233 50 33
www.degrootewittearend.be

Here is a beautiful old café located in a town house that goes back to the 15th century. In the summer months, you can drink a Belgian beer at a long wooden bench in the renaissance courtyard while classical music plays in the background.

140 BIER CENTRAL

De Keyserlei 25
Station Quarter ④
+32 (0)3 201 59 85
www.biercentral.be

Davy Verbeke opened this specialised beer café near central station as a homage to Belgian beer. The choice is exceptional, with 20 varieties on tap and some 300 bottled beers listed in a thick beer menu. You can see the most exclusive bottles stacked in the cellar as you head for the toilets.

The 5 most
ROMANTIC CAFES

---

141 SHILLING
Graaf van Egmont-
straat 60
Het Zuid ②
+32 (0)3 257 76 78
www.cafeshilling.be

This handsome café decorated with black and green tiles and old wooden doors is one of many new bars and restaurants created by Vinko Pepa. Decorated with brown chesterfield sofas and chairs, oriental rugs and potted palms, it has the feel of a colonial club.

142 SYMFOROSA
Vleminckveld 18
Central Antwerp ①
+32 (0)3 233 84 09
www.symforosa.com

This café occupies a grand old house with an impressive entrance hall. It feels much more intimate once you are inside, with three small rooms decorated with black tables, flowers and little candles in jars. The kitchen offers simple wholesome food, including homemade soup, salads or quiche.

143 MELKERIJ
Nachtegalenpark
Floraliënlaan 115
Suburbs (Middelheim)⑬
+32 (0)3 828 93 81
www.melkerij-
nachtegalenpark.be

This rustic thatched café is buried away in a wooded country estate to the south of Antwerp. Built as a dairy, it was converted into a café in the 1920s. The spacious main room has large windows, a big fireplace and a painted ceiling. It is surrounded by a large terrace shaded by old trees.

144 CARAVAN
Damplein 17
Antwerpen-Noord ⑨
+32 (0)3 297 68 52

Located in a former pharmacy, this is a relaxed corner café that appeals to young families and artists. The kitchen offers a *koppijnontbijt*, or hangover breakfast, which comes with a choice of a beer or an aspirin. Or you can order a picnic hamper to take to the park, complete with checked tablecloth.

145 ESCO*BAR
Quellinstraat 32
Station Quarter ④
+32 (0)3 336 18 11
www.koffieenlunchescobar.be

Located in a busy street near the station, this coffee bar is the coolest place around. Run by a friendly young couple, it offers a range of coffees made with the best beans, along with cakes and sandwiches. The interior has a vintage look, while the back garden is a rare treat in this area of town.

141 SHILLING

The 5 best
WINE BARS

---

146 PAZZO
Oudeleeuwenrui 12
University Quarter ③
+32 (0)3 232 86 82
www.pazzo.be

This modern wine bar and restaurant is located in a former warehouse in the old port quarter. It is run by Willem Wouters, whose wife Filipa Pato is one of Portugal's leading winemakers. Together they have built up an exceptional cellar that runs to 170 different wines. The list includes bottles from Filipa's family vineyard in Óis do Bairro.

147 PATINE
Leopold de Waelstraat 1
Het Zuid ②
+32 (0)3 257 09 19
www.wijnbistropatine.be

It's easy to spot this deeply romantic wine bistro. Just stand outside the Royal Fine Arts Museum and look for the building with the green and yellow tiled façade. This mellow, candlelit restaurant is the perfect place to share a bottle of wine. Breakfast is also served here.

148 VIGNETO
Wijngaardstraat 5
Central Antwerp ①
+32 (0)3 345 95 65

This new wine bar located on a quiet cobbled street in the historic centre has a striking modern interior. The owners have put together an inspired list of 20 wines that can be ordered by the glass, accompanied by a plate of sliced Italian ham.

149 **VINICITY**
Karel Rogierstraat 40
Het Zuid ②
+32 (0)3 345 33 44
www.vinicity.com

This ecological wine bar is located on a corner opposite the Royal Fine Arts Museum. The interior is a relaxed mix of recycled wood and black wine racks. The sommelier selects nine wines every week that are served by the glass while the kitchen offers an inspiring range of tapas as early evening nibbles.

150 **VINO-TEKA**
Cassierstraat 41
Antwerpen-Noord ⑨
+32 (0)3 770 75 55
www.vinoteka.be

This relaxed little wine bar lies away from the tourist haunts near Park Spoor Noord. Owners Bart Huybrechts and Steven Alaerts offer some exceptional finds and also occasionally organise food tastings, concerts and even now and then a neighbourhood street party.

The 5 best
COFFEE BARS

---

151 CAFFÈNATION
Mechelsesteenweg 16
Central Antwerp ①
+32 (0)486 32 30 15
www.caffenation.be

This relaxed, friendly coffee bar is popular with young urban nomads tapping on laptops or reading *De Morgen*. Owner Rob Berghmans imports the finest beans he can find, selling them to other coffee shops such as Coffee & Vinyl. A second Caffènation at Hopland 46 serves takeaway coffee.

152 NORMO
Minderbroedersrui 30
Central Antwerp ①
www.normocoffee.com

Here is a friendly espresso bar where art school students rub shoulders with the old lady in a coat who has dropped in with her dog. The interior is the familiar ramshackle Antwerp mix of brick walls, ancient armchairs and art magazines.

153 BROER BRETEL
Nassaustraat 7
Het Eilandje ⑧
+32 (0)484 15 82 96
www.broerbretel.be

This is a great little coffee bar close to the MAS museum. It has two small rooms furnished in 1950s vintage style. Cool jazz plays in the background as the two friendly baristas create ever more sophisticated coffees. In case you were wondering about the name, it means Brother Braces.

154 **KOLONEL KOFFIE**
   Grote Pieter Potstraat 38
   Central Antwerp ①
   +32 (0)486 65 51 55
   www.kolonelkoffie.be

Kobe Van Gaveren and Femke Nuyens opened this friendly coffee bar in 2012 in an old street near the river. They were inspired by the coffee culture of Australia, so the atmosphere is informal, with vintage tables and chairs dotted around. The upper floor is one of our favourite secret spots.

155 **CAFEMATIC**
   Vleminckveld 4
   Central Antwerp ①
   +32 (0)3 225 59 55
   www.cafematicantwerpen.be

A friendly cafe on a little square filled with parked bikes. The interior is pure vintage chic, with black-and-white tiled floor, period lamps and old school classroom chairs. Good coffee and tasty sandwiches are served by friendly staff while music plays quietly in the background.

151 CAFFENATION

The 5 best
COCKTAIL BARS

---

156 COCKTAILS AT NINE
Lijnwaadmarkt 9
Central Antwerp ①
+ 32 (0)3 707 10 07
www.cocktailsatnine.be

This cocktail bar near the Cathedral is an appealing place to spend an evening. Located in a historic building, it has stone floors, leather sofas and a blazing fire. The barman knows how to mix a cocktail and the little back courtyard is the perfect spot to catch the sun.

157 SIPS
Gillisplaats 8
Het Zuid ②
+32 (0)3 257 39 59
www.sips-cocktails.com

After serving cocktails for 12 years on the Queen Elizabeth II liner, Manuel Wouters opened a cocktail bar in Antwerp's south side. It's a stylish, modern place that draws a well-dressed crowd. The cocktails are made using old recipes that often go back centuries.

158 VIBES
Grote Pieter Potstraat 14
Central Antwerp ①
+32 (0)484 942 644
www.vibeshouse.be

Located in an old brick building near the Scheldt, Vibes is a relaxed place to drink cocktails while the DJs play an eclectic blend of music. The bar has a regular programme of events including live bands that play in the vaulted cellar.

159 JOSEPHINE'S

Gentplaats 1
Het Zuid ②
+32 (0)3 248 95 95
www.josephines.be

Here is a romantic place for an evening out, starting with a cocktail. The interior is decorated in 1950s living room style. The drinks menu includes Martinis flavoured with a hint of fruit and spices. The place fills up on Fridays and Saturdays when the resident DJs spin a mix of jazz and soul.

160 MAMA MATREA

Lange Nieuwstraat 13
Central Antwerp ①
+32 (0)487 23 26 44
www.mamamatrea.com

This friendly cocktail bar attracts a multicultural crowd with its cheap cocktails, healthy cooking and party atmosphere. The bar hosts events including open mic sessions with urban poets on occasional Tuesdays.

The 5 best café terraces for
SITTING IN THE SUN

---

161 **BARNINI**
Oudevaartplaats 10
Central Antwerp ①
+32 (0)3 485 82 69

A friendly coffee bar with a homely vintage interior and a random collection of tables and chairs spreading out onto the pavement. You can even wrap yourself in a blanket if it is chilly. The café exhibits works by local artists and photographers. The food can sometimes be slow to arrive, so don't come here if you are in a rush.

162 **KAPITEIN ZEPPOS**
Vleminckveld 78
Central Antwerp ①
+32 (0)3 231 17 89
www.cafezeppos.be

Named after a TV programme that Belgian kids watched in the 1960s, this is a relaxed café and restaurant with bare brick walls, old wooden tables and the menu chalked on a blackboard. In the summer, the vast terrace with its distinctive red chairs is the perfect spot to sit with a Leffe.

163 **MIKA**
Middelheimlaan 63
Suburbs (Middelheim) ⑬
+32 (0)470 531 154
www.mi-ka.be

The museum café at Middelheim Park is located in an old country house surrounded by a moat. You can drink a beer on the terrace shaded by ancient trees, or sit inside on a sofa looking out on the water.

164 **DE BIOLOGISCH-DYNAMISCHE BAKKERIJ**
Mechelsesteenweg 72
Southern Antwerp ⑦
+32 (0)3 216 00 42

Carlos Maldonado hit on a successful formula when he opened a bio bakery/café in the Volkstraat, so he went on to open a second branch. The back garden is a lovely overgrown corner where you can sit in the summer at a metal table eating a delicious sandwich made with homemade bread.

165 **LLOYD LOOM**
Bakkerssteegje
Groendalstraat 18
Central Antwerp ①
+32 (0)3 232 69 54
www.lloydloom.eu

Here is one of the most hidden courtyards in downtown Antwerp, reached down a narrow alley that runs between old whitewashed houses. You turn a final corner and enter a leafy courtyard with some tables set out. The perfect place to stop for coffee and cheesecake.

163 MIKA

The 5 best cafés for
FREE WIFI

---

166 **REVISTA**
Karel Rogierstraat 47
Het Zuid ②
+32 (0)486 07 25 62

Located near the Royal Fine Arts Museum, this is a hotspot for the creative laptop nomads. You can check your emails while the barista prepares a perfect Illy espresso, or flick through one of the international art and design magazines. We are told that the artist Luc Tuymans likes to drop in here.

167 **KUBUS PERMEKE**
De Coninckplein 25
Antwerpen-Noord ⑨
+ 32 (0)3 338 38 00
www.permeke.org

The city library moved in 2005 to a former Ford garage on the edge of the Chinatown district. The architects have preserved the car ramp inside the building as a computer zone You can also use the free wifi in the library café Kubus, which occupies a striking glass cube overlooking the renovated square De Coninckplein.

168 **BERLIN**
Kleine Markt 1
Central Antwerp ①
+32 (0)3 227 11 01
www.brasserieberlin.be

This crowded café-brasserie is maybe not the quietest place to tap out an email, but it is one of the few cafés in central Antwerp that offer free wifi. The black walls and steel air ducts create a hard edge reminiscent of a Berlin bar.

169 **UFO**
Waalse Kaai 47
Het Zuid ②
+32 (0)470 69 11 80
www.ufocafe.be

Here is a cool new museum café decorated with pale wood furniture, vast mirrors and candles. The terrace outside is sheltered by a low hedge, making it a seductive spot on a summer evening.

170 **THE SQUARE**
Koningin Astridplein 7
Station Quarter ④
+32 (0)3 203 12 34
www.parkplaza.com

This quiet hotel bar belongs to the Radisson Blu Astrid opposite Central Station. It's hard to find anyone in Antwerp who likes the building, which resembles a Disney resort hotel, but the hotel bar is a relaxed spot where the coffee comes with a glass of liqueur and wifi is free.

'T STAD LEEST

40 PLACES TO SHOP

The 5 most
UNUSUAL SHOPS

---

171 **STEEN & BEEN**
Volkstraat 59
Het Zuid ②
+32 (0)3 237 25 22
www.steenenbeen.be

This exotic shop sells marvels made from steen en been (stone and bone). Among the natural wonders are gorgeous seashells, frail bird skeletons and vivid butterflies in wooden frames. The objects are beautifully displayed like objects in an 18th century cabinet of curiosities.

172 **MIDDELHEIM MUSEUM SHOP**
Middelheimlaan 61
Suburbs (Middelheim) ⑫
+32 (0)3 288 33 60
www.middelheimmuseum.be

Here is a fun place to buy postcards, art books, magazines, T-shirts and bags. The interior was designed by the Ghent architects aNNo who came up with the neat idea of constructing the counter and shelves out of stacked books.

173 **INTERNATIONAL MAGAZINE STORE** 1
Melkmarkt 17
Central Antwerp ①
+32 (0)3 233 16 88
www.imstijdschriften.be

The shelves in this store are crammed with 10,000 different magazines and newspapers from all over the world. The stock includes more than 30 different tattoo magazines and every language edition of *Cosmopolitan*, along with obscure art magazines. The Gothic arches are all that remains of a mediaeval chapel that once stood on the site.

174 INTERNATIONAL MAGAZINE STORE 2

Meir 78
Central Antwerp ①
+32 (0)3 227 46 81
www.imstijdschriften.nl

The International Magazine Store opened a new branch in 2011 in the renovated Stadsfeestzaal. On the shelves are some 10,000 different magazines, newspapers and books. We come here regularly because it's the only place in Belgium that stocks *Frankie* magazine.

175 MEKANIK STRIP

Sint-Jacobsmarkt 73
University Quarter ③
+32 (0)3 234 2347
www.mekanik-strip.be

Here is comic books heaven. Connoisseurs of Marvel comics need look no further. All the Tintin books are here, along with shelves of Manga and the odd book by the Brussels illustrator Ever Meulen. A little back room is filled with figurines and the first floor is used for exhibitions.

171 STEEN EN BEEN

The 5 best
INDEPENDENT
BOOKSHOPS

---

176 DE GROENE WATERMAN

Wolstraat 7
Central Antwerp ①
+32 (0)3 232 93 94
www.groenewaterman.be

A beautiful bookshop with a mysterious name (The Green Waterman) that no one seems able to explain. Most books are in Dutch, but it has some English fiction, including Flemish literature in translation. They also stock Believer, McSweeny's and indeed anything with Dave Eggers' name attached. Children's books are kept in a room at the back.

177 COPYRIGHT

Nationalestraat 28
Central Antwerp ①
+ 32 (0)3 232 94 16
www.copyrightbookshop.be

Here is a seriously stylish bookshop designed by the Antwerp architect Vincent Van Duysen in 2000. Located in the same building as the fashion museum, it has a striking interior with white walls, black bookshelves and two low tables piled with gorgeous art and architecture books.

178 'T STAD LEEST

Steenhouwersvest 16
Central Antwerp ①
+32 (0)3 233 08 80
www.tstadleest.be

This spacious, independent bookshop opened in an Antwerp townhouse in 2011. It stocks beautiful Taschen art books, cookbooks and children's fiction. It also has Moleskine notebooks, quirky games and unusual postcards.

179 ALTA VIA

Nassaustraat 29
Het Eilandje ⑧
+32 (0)3 293 87 33
www.altaviatravelbooks.be

Here is a bookshop in the docks quarter where you can equip yourself for a globe-trotting adventure. As well as a large stock of travel guides, it sells hiking maps, illuminated globes and trekking equipment. The furniture was made using recycled wooden crates.

180 OTHELLO

Handschoenmarkt 3
Central Antwerp ①
+32 (0)3 689 23 53

This new bookshop opened in 2012 on a little square facing the Cathedral. Occupying the ground floor of a design hotel, it has black walls and large display tables. The stock includes a large section of English fiction, along with art books, travel guides and postcards.

177 COPYRIGHT

The 5 best
INDEPENDENT RECORD STORES

181 **TUNE UP**
Melkmarkt 17
Central Antwerp ①
+32 (0)3 226 84 11
www.tuneuprecords.com

Here is a serious little record store hidden away above a magazine shop. The records are neatly arranged in old crates according to genre, while the walls are crammed with posters and art. The two owners are fanatical about music. They also serve coffee and things to nibble.

182 **COFFEE & VINYL**
Volkstraat 45
Het Zuid ②
+ 32 (0)3 337 77 93
www.coffeeandvinyl.com

A nostalgic record shop which also serves coffee. The owner Lars Cosemans sells vintage records in the back room and coffee in the front area, which is furnished with colourful metal chairs and school desks. The paintings on the wall are by young Antwerp artists.

183 **FAT KAT RECORDS**
Lange Koepoortstraat 51
Central Antwerp ①
+32 (0)3 232 09 41
www.fatkat.be

Here is a shop where you can find recordings by the most obscure alternative bands. The stock includes new releases and vintage vinyl. And if you can't find what you want, the owner is happy to order it. You can also buy concert tickets here.

184 RECORD COLLECTOR

Lange Koepoortstraat 70
Central Antwerp ⓘ
+32 (0)3 252 56 26

Vinyl junkies can easily spend half a day in Record Collector searching through the boxes of old LPs going back to the 1950s. Some of the records are exceedingly rare and quite pricey, but there are bargains in the back room.

185 CHELSEA RECORDS

Kloosterstraat 10
Central Antwerp ⓘ
+32 (0)3 233 85 77

It's a tight squeeze in this little shop on the Kloosterstraat. The owner has filled every available space with records and CDs which are classified according to the artist's first name. It can be difficult to find anything, but the owner can point you in the right direction.

The 5 best shops for
UNUSUAL GIFTS

---

186 PLANTIN MORETUS MUSEUM SHOP

Vrijdagmarkt 22-23
Central Antwerp ①
+32 (0)3 221 14 50
www.museumplantin-
moretus.be

The Plantin Moretus Museum opened a new shop in 2010 where they sell postcards, books, maps, prints and note-books. You can pick up some unusual gifts here, including miniature globes, framed botanical illustrations and book-marks illustrated with a 16th century view of Antwerp.

187 LENA & ZASA

Transvaalstraat 75
Zurenborg ⑥
+32 (0)3 218 50 24
www.lenazasa.com

This bright corner shop is the place to come if you are looking for something different. It sells jewellery, bags, compu-ter gadgets and odd accessories. You can also find interesting children's toys like a wooden robot kit.

188 MAS SHOP

Hanzestedenplaats 1
Het Eilandje ⑧
+32 (0)3 337 59 48
www.masshop.be

The museum shop next to MAS occupies a low building on the waterfront clad in the same livid red sandstone as the museum. Here you can buy art books, nautical maps, docklands guides, amusing postcards, Antwerp T-shirts and branded mugs.

189 **AKOTEE**

Melkmarkt 28
Central Antwerp ①
+32 (0)3 213 23 13
www.akotee.be

Akotee and its two sister shops on Melkmarkt sell bright childish stuff, like floral-print bike saddle bags, wooden reindeer wall mounts and kitsch laptop bags. Nothing is too serious.

190 **ROOMS**

Sint-Katelijnevest 52
Central Antwerp ①
+32 (0)3 336 35 36
www.rooms-shop.be

A vintage caravan is parked in the window of this quirky shop where they sells fun utensils for the home and garden. You will find sophisticated fish tanks designed to look like modern houses, eccentric clocks and colourful gadgets.

189 AKOTEE

The 5 best
BIKE SHOPS

---

191 DE GEUS

Geuzenstraat 37
Het Zuid ②
+32 (0)3 238 17 12
www.fietsendegeus.be

This helpful bike shop mainly stocks classic Dutch bike made by Gazelle or Batavus, but also a range of Brompton folding bikes, along with baby seats, helmets and loud bells. They also do repairs and have installed a free air pump outside, to the left of the entrance.

192 FIETS!

Vlaamse Kaai 20
Het Zuid ②
+32 (0)3 337 66 98
www.fiets.be

This spacious shop on two floors is where fashionable Zuid residents shop for city bikes, folding bikes to take on the train or the latest electric models. This store also stocks satellite navigation systems, designer saddle bags and hip Nutcase helmets.

193 DE VELODROME

Dageraadplaats 34
Zurenborg ⑥
+32 (0)3 236 22 37
www.develodrome.be

Former racing cyclist Tom Teck runs this bike shop in the fashionable Zurenborg district. He sells racing bikes, city bikes, bells, helmets and bags. He also repairs bikes and organises cycle trips twice a week through the Antwerp countryside.

194 FIXERATI

Lange Koepoortstraat 13
Central Antwerp ①
+32 (0)3 227 33 13
www.bikeproject.be

Daan Terclavers runs a friendly bike shop in the city centre with the latest bikes, clothes and locks. He has everything from solid city bikes to cool racing models. He also sells second-hand bikes and does repairs in his workshop right in the middle of the shop.

195 DYNAMO

Kasteelpleinstraat 57
Central Antwerp ①
+32 (0)3 232 87 08

You can't miss the bright orange façade of this friendly bike shop. It sells sturdy bikes for daily commuting on the Antwerp cobbles as well as racing models and kids' bikes. You can also pick up accessories like saddle bags, bells and locks.

191 DE GEUS

The 5 best
STREET MARKETS

196 VRIJDAGMARKT
Vrijdagmarkt
Central Antwerp ①
Fridays 09.00 to 13.00

People have been coming to the street auction on the Vrijdagmarkt since the 16th century. Here is where dealers sell off old office furniture from firms that have just gone bankrupt, ornaments that once belonged to someone's grandmother, and plastic bin bags filled with miscellaneous junk.

197 VOGELENMARKT
Oudevaartplaats
Central Antwerp ①
Sundays 08.00 to 13.00

The Vogelenmarkt is a raucous street market with its origins in a 16th century poultry market on the Meir. It relocated in 1912 to its current location, where stallholders sell fruit, flowers, street food and clothes. A handful of dealers still sell small caged birds in a corner of the market.

198 ZATERDAGMARKT
Theaterplein
Central Antwerp ①
Saturdays 08.00 to 16.00

Antwerp's multicultural food market is held under a huge glass canopy on the Theaterplein. Stallholders sell fruit from Limburg and fish from Ostend, alongside exotic street food from North Africa, Asia and Turkey.

199 MARKT VAN MORGEN
Kloosterstraat
Central Antwerp ①
www.marktvanmorgen.be

Young Antwerp designers set up stalls at the south end of Kloosterstraat on certain Sundays in the summer. It's worth coming just to wander around listening to some cool band playing in the background while nibbling on a cupcake from a brightly-painted caravan parked on the street.

200 BOEKENMART
De Coninckplein
Antwerpen-Noord ⑨
Every third Sunday
of the month,
10.00 to 16.00

A relaxed monthly market on the square outside the city library where stallholders sell old books, vinyl records and street food. A pleasant place to spend a Sunday morning browsing among dusty books.

197 VOGELENMARKT

The 5 best
FLOWER SHOPS

---

201 BALTIMORE
Orgelstraat 6
Central Antwerp ①
+32 (0)3 232 28 38
www.baltimorebloemen.be

Marc Colle creates the most flamboyant bouquets using rare flowers. In recent years, he has created floral displays for several Antwerp designers, including Dries van Noten, Ann Demeulemeester and Raf Simons. Yet his bouquets are still remarkably affordable.

202 FIORI
Quellinstraat 45
Station Quarter ④
+32 (0)3 233 86 82
www.atelier-vivaldi.be

This shop sells plants to brighten up offices in the diamond district. It has a wide selection of beautiful orchids, but also sells sturdy outdoor plants for urban balconies and beautiful bouquets to take to a dinner party.

203 DITO
Sint-Jorispoort 30
Central Antwerp ①
+32 (0)3 293 95 19
www.dito-antwerp.be

This tiny shop filled with flowers occupies a historic house in the old town. The owner suggests simple arrangements like a bunch of yellow tulips or a pot with three hyacinths. He also sells potted plants for balconies, or even a single cut rose for Valentine's Day.

204 DE GROENE DROOM

Kasteelpleinstraat 51
Central Antwerp ①
+32 (0)3 232 26 47
www.degroenedroom.be

This smart shop has giant cacti in the window and bright cut flowers arranged in old zinc pots on two long shelves. The shop will sell you plants for a roof terrace, or put together a bouquet for your best friend's wedding.

205 FLOR ARTES

Mechelsesteenweg 159
Southern Antwerp ⑦
+32 (0)3 230 82 14
www.florartes.be

The brothers Yvan and Sven Roelandts opened this flower shop in 1985. They have an enormous variety of cut flowers sitting in metal pots along with exotic plants for living rooms and urban terraces.

203 **DITO**

The 5 best shops for
ANTIQUES and
OLD BOOKS

---

206 'T KOETSHUIS
Kloosterstraat 62
Central Antwerp ①
+32 (0)3 248 33 42

This cluttered shop on two floors is packed with furniture, ornaments, vases, postcards, lamps, typewriters, posters and old magazines. China dolls that were once a child's most precious possession are now sold for a few euro.

207 46 KLOOSTERSTRAAT
Kloosterstraat 46
Central Antwerp ①
+32 (0)477 97 75 32
www.46kloosterstraat.com

This chaotic corner shop has been selling strange objects from all corners of the world since 1988. You will find Fifties chairs, anatomy charts, ornamental cats and old shop mannequins, all thrown together with no sense of order.

208 DEMIAN BOOKS
Hendrik Conscience-plein 16-18
Central Antwerp ①
+32 (0)3 233 32 48
www.demian.be

René Franken has been running this appealing second-hand bookshop built into the walls of the Carolus Borromeus church for more than 20 years. He plays cool jazz as he sorts through the piles of discarded books and publishes occasional books on themes that interest him.

209 **ERIK TONEN**

Kloosterstraat 48
Central Antwerp ①
+32 (0)495 25 35 66
www.erik-tonen-books.be

Erik Tonen sells rare old books in a beautiful wood-panelled shop on Kloosterstraat. Displayed on the tables are art books, photography books and books about Antwerp. The glass cabinets contain rare books including the occasional 15th century illuminated manuscript.

210 **FRED & ZORRO**

Sint-Jorispoort 7
Central Antwerp ①
+32 (0)477 62 98 51

Fred Van Der Voort sells vintage furniture from the 1950s and 1960s as well as contemporary design. Anyone looking for an authentic Eames chair has come to the right place.

210 FRED & ZORRO

HOSPITAL

50 PLACES FOR FASHION AND DESIGN

———

The 5 best shops for
ANTWERP FASHION

211 **LOUIS**
Lombardenstraat 2
Central Antwerp ①
+32 (0)3 232 98 72

Geert Bruloot opened this shop in 1986 to sell clothes by the Antwerp Six. Now run by Marjan Eggers, the shop still stocks clothes by the best designers, including Ann Demeulemeester, Martin Margiela and Dior, but it also promotes young talent by inviting final year fashion students to exhibit in the window.

212 **DVS**
Schuttershofstraat 9
Central Antwerp ①

No name. Nothing. Most people don't know this shop exists. The shop is on the first floor in a former atelier once occupied by Walter van Beirendonck. His partner, Dirk Van Saene (one of the original Antwerp Six) opened this shop in 2013. Van Saene sells his own clothes along with fashion by Sophie D'Hoore, Veronique Branquinho and Van Beirendonck.

213 **HET MODEPALEIS**
Nationalestraat 16
Central Antwerp ①
+32 (0)3 470 25 10
www.driesvannoten.be

Dries Van Noten renovated the 19th century Modepaleis in 1989 as his flagship store. Furnished with wooden cabinets and vintage leather chairs, this is where the quiet Antwerp designer displays his sober, often melancholy collections.

214 ANN DEMEULEMEESTER

Leopold De Waelplaats
Het Zuid ②
+32 (0)3 216 01 33
www.anndemeulemeester.be

Born in 1959, Ann Demeulemeester is the most serious of the Antwerp Six. She likes black. She likes leather. She is a big fan of Patti Smith. She sells her cool minimalist fashion in a large corner building with raw wooden floors, white walls and a salvaged wooden beam used to display shoes.

215 ANNA HEYLEN

Lombardenstraat 16
Central Antwerp ①
+32 (0)3 213 01 60
www.annaheylen.be

A graduate of the Antwerp Academy, Anna Heylen made her name in 1993 with an eerie exhibition of life-sized hanging dolls in the abandoned Sint-Felix warehouse. She has her workshop above the Antwerp store and occasionally comes downstairs to talk to customers.

211 LOUIS

The 5 hippest

HIGH FASHION BOUTIQUES

216 CAFÉ COSTUME

Emiel Banningstraat 11
Het Zuid ②
+32 (0)3 257 30 02
www.cafecostume.com

In a discreet shop on the south side of the city, Bruno Van Gils and his two nieces offer affordable bespoke tailoring in a vintage interior dotted with family mementoes. You start by making an appointment. Then you sit in a handsome room to discuss your needs. Three weeks later, you return to the fitting room for the final touches.

217 STEP BY STEP

Lombardenvest 18
Central Antwerp ①
+32 (0)3 213 18 54
www.stepbystep-antwerpen.be

The owners of this upmarket fashion shop grab people's attention with their window displays. Nicole Kidman noticed the shop window when she was in Antwerp and dropped in to browse and buy. The clothes on the racks are by designers like Isabel Marant, Alexander Wang and Marcel de Bruxelles.

218 SEVEN ROOMS

Sint-Antoniusstraat 12
Central Antwerp ①
+32 (0)3 227 12 00
www.sevenrooms.be

Gustav Bruynseraede's second shop is just as original as his first. While XSO (Eiermarkt 13) had a Japanese purity, Seven Rooms is like your cool friend's Berlin loft, divided into a living room, bar, kitchen and library. In this clean domestic space you can buy stylish clothes and accessories, along with art.

219 ANJA SCHWERBROCK

Kloosterstraat 175
Central Antwerp ①
+32 (0)3 237 38 67
www.anjaschwerbrock.com

The young German designer Anja Schwerbrock designs her own collections which she sells in a small Antwerp shop. She studied with Issey Miyake in Tokyo before settling in Antwerp and likes to work with single colours – mainly black and white – to create sublime dresses, sweaters and bags.

220 VERSO

Lange Gasthuisstraat 9
Central Antwerp ①
+32 (0)3 226 92 92
www.verso.be

Based in two 16th century buildings once occupied by the Deutsche Bank, this upmarket shop sells clothes by luxury brands like Dolce & Gabbana, Armani and Helmut Lang. The café is a stylish place for lunch while the impressive toilets are located in the vaults of the former bank.

The 5 best
FASHION SHOPS FOR WOMEN

---

221 **FRESH 34**
Volkstraat 34
Het Zuid ②

This little store in Het Zuid is the place to shop if you are looking for that chic Parisian look. The friendly owner selects some beautiful clothes and accessories by brands like Sessùn, April 77 and Marie Sixtine.

222 **BABY BELUGA**
Volkstraat 1
Het Zuid ②
+32 (0)3 289 90 60
www.babybeluga.be

This corner shop sets out to be a little bit naughty. So the walls are painted deep red and black, like a Victorian brothel, while the clothes and accessories are sexy and sensual. It's just the spot to find a dress to wear to a wild party in a docklands warehouse.

223 **ATELIER ASSEMBLE**
Leopold de Waelstraat 30
Het Zuid ②
+32 (0)3 216 03 06
www.assemble.be

The women who run Atelier Assemblé create beautiful, original clothes out of vintage fabrics dating from the 1950s to 1970s. The shop has a sober 1950s interior with racks of old fabrics that can be turned into brand new, exclusive clothes for kids and women.

224 GARDE-ROBE NATIONALE

Nationalestraat 72
Central Antwerp ①
+32 (0)3 485 86 87
www.garde-robe-nationale.be

Designer Nathalie Lachat sells Belgian fashion in a beautiful interior - the space at the front is brightly lit while the back room is dark and mysterious. Here you can find clothes by Tim Van Steenbergen, Sandrina Fasoli and Just in Case, as well as Nathalie's own label Magdalena.

225 SIENNA & LOIS

Kammenstraat 89
Central Antwerp ①
+32 (0)3 234 21 03

This friendly new boutique on Kammenstraat sells urban fashion in a sober vintage interior. The shop stocks relatively inexpensive clothes, shoes and accessories by chic French brands like Deby Debo and 2Two.

The 5 best shops for
ANTWERP STREET STYLE

---

226 FISH & CHIPS
Kammenstraat 26
Central Antwerp ①
+32 (0)3 227 08 24
www.fishandchips.be

This cool fashion store has lost some of its edge, but it still has the wildest window displays. It stocks Vans, skater gear, T-shirts, art books and labels that are not easy to find anywhere else. The best time to shop is on a Saturday when a Belgian DJ plays tracks in a little booth perched above the store.

227 WHO'S THAT GIRL
Drukkerijstraat 16
Central Antwerp ①
+32 (0)3 248 07 82
www.whosthatgirl.eu

Two Antwerp designers created this fun retro label based on girly bright colours, polka dots and a 1950s mood. In 2013 the shop moved into a new interior decorated with retro furniture and lighting by Tom Dixon.

228 FANS
Kammenstraat 80
Central Antwerp ①
+32 (0)3 232 31 72
www.fanssite.be

This shop imported British punk style to Antwerp in the 1970s. It used to be seen as a den of vice, but has now blended into the Kammenstraat scene. So here is where young people can find heavy metal T-shirts, vampire capes, Harry Potter wands, purple wigs and kinky corsets.

229 THE PUBLIC IMAGE

Wijngaardstraat 16
Central Antwerp ①
+32 (0)484 80 02 26
www.thepublicimage.be

Nele Moens runs this hip store where you find fashion by emerging designers hard to locate anywhere else in Belgium. The stock includes boots by Jeffrey Campbell and jewellery by Melody Ehsani, along with a small selection of vintage clothes.

230 LUX STREETFASHION

Kipdorpvest 36
Central Antwerp ①
+32 (0)3 225 24 09

Mo Azhir used to play basketball for the Antwerp Giants, but now runs this cool shoe shop stocked with a huge range of sneakers by brands like Nike, Supra and Jordan. Mo also sells bright T-shirts and baseball caps by famous teams like the Red Sox and the Yankees.

The 5 best
VINTAGE SHOPS

---

231 THINK TWICE

Lange Klarenstraat 21
Central Antwerp ①
www.thinktwice-
secondhand.be

The Finnish second-hand chain Think Twice now has four branches in Antwerp where they sell glamorous vintage dresses, shoes and bags. Look out on their Facebook page for T2 special promotions when they sell off everything in stock at prices that make no economic sense. By the third day, you can pick up stuff for just one euro.

232 JUTKA EN RISKA

Nationalestraat 87
Central Antwerp ①
+32 (0)473 52 82 52

A cool vintage shop aimed at sophisticated women looking for inexpensive designer clothes and offbeat accessories. The friendly people who work here can help you find your way around. It may take no more than a €10 note to obtain the wildest sunglasses you have ever worn.

233 LABELS INC.

Aalmoezenierstraat 4
Central Antwerp ①
+32 (0)3 232 60 56
www.labelsinc.be

This shop sells clothes from past seasons by famous names in Flemish fashion, including the Antwerp Six and Martin Margiela, as well as a few international designers. The window display features new work by students from the Antwerp fashion academy.

234 FOXHOLE

Reyndersstraat 10
Central Antwerp ①
www.foxholeshop.com

Here is a vintage shop in the heart of the fashion district that sells some classy clothes including dresses, hats, belts and shoes. Nothing stays on the racks for more than a month and the window display is constantly refreshed. Two other branches are located in downtown Brussels.

235 SUSSIES

Oude Koornmarkt 69
Central Antwerp ①
+32 (0)3 608 63 51
www.sussiesvintage.nl

Located in a side street near Groenplaats, this Dutch vintage shop sells beautiful dresses, chunky sweaters, wild sunglasses and slightly worn shoes, as well as designer tables and odd 1960s lamps. You can sit in the café listening to cool background music while you update your blog.

232 JUTKA EN RISKA

The 5 most innovative
CONCEPT STORES

---

236 **GRAANMARKT 13**
Graanmarkt 13
Central Antwerp ①
+32 (0)3 337 79 92
www.graanmarkt13.be

This is one of the most stylish shops in Antwerp, with an art gallery, a shop and a restaurant. The shop is filled with interesting and unusual brands. Young Belgian chef Seppe Nobels provides the honest cooking that Antwerp fashionistas crave.

237 **RA**
Kleine Markt 7-9
Central Antwerp ①
+32 (0)3 292 37 80
www.ra13.be

An intriguing shop with two floors of fashion, a bookshop, art gallery, sculpture garden, café and thatched-roof office. The emphasis here is on sustainable clothes and craftsmanship. The relaxed bohemian café with its flea market furniture and mismatched crockery is Antwerp at its most cool.

238 **YOUR**
Kloosterstraat 90
Central Antwerp ①
+32 (0)3 337 71 10
www.your-antwerp.com

Here you can buy everything from a tiny pack of €2 bubblegum to a luxury car costing €200,000. They also have a resident hairdresser, perfume consultant, coffee bar and their own newspaper. The staff here are exceptionally friendly, especially Barbara down in the men's department.

239 HOSPITAL

De Burburestraat 4
Het Zuid ②
+32 (0)3 311 89 80
www.hospital-antwerp.com

Here is a stunning concept store located in stables that once belonged to a hippodrome. The interior was given a quirky makeover by the Pure Sang agency to create an intriguing retail space featuring exposed brick, Moorish tiles and glass panels. The store stocks high fashion by international brands.

240 MOOSE IN THE CITY

IJzerenwaag 10
Central Antwerp ①
+32 (0)3 369 12 12
www.moose-in-the-city.com

The owners of this cool contemporary store sell some stylish Scandinavian stuff. You can buy thick woollen sweaters, Nordic crime fiction, hiking equipment, Filippa K shirts and Muuto light bulbs. Should you want to set off on an outdoors Scandinavian adventure, the trip can be booked here.

239 HOSPITAL

237 RA

The 5 best
SHOE SHOPS

241 **COCCODRILLO**

Schuttershofstraat 9
Central Antwerp ①
+32 (0)3 233 20 93
www.coccodrillo.be

In a city of cobbled streets, it makes no sense to wear expensive high heels. But Antwerp women don't care. They leave Coccodrillo with footwear designed by the likes of Prada, Dries Van Noten and Maison Martin Margiela. Men can drop into the branch of Coccodrillo across the street, furnished in the style of a 1930s Buenos Aires salon.

242 **ALLEZ-Y**

Groendalstraat 6
Central Antwerp ①
+32 (0)3 231 11 57

Yvette Van Riel sells cool shoes and sandals for young women in a bare white interior that could almost be an art gallery. As well as international brands, she sells her own collection called Euforie made by skilled Italian craftsmen.

243 **MONAR**

Lombardenvest 61
Central Antwerp ①
+32 (0)3 225 05 20
www.monar.be

This upmarket store stocks smart designer shoes for men and women. The collections include footwear by Maison Martin Margiela, Paul Smith, Converse and Vans. They also stock bags, satchels and bracelets.

244 ELSA

Nationalestraat 147
Central Antwerp ①
+32 (0)3 226 84 54
www.elsa-antwerp.be

Els Proost worked for Armani and Dries van Noten before opening a shop in Antwerp selling shoes and bags. She launched her own collection in 2007 in which she combines the craft she learned in Italy with the creative flair that comes from living in Antwerp.

245 THIRON

Drukkerijstraat 6
Central Antwerp ①
+32 (0)3 227 20 27
www.thiron.be

Guy Thiron was an industrial designer before he discovered that his real passion lay in shoes. He sells beautiful well-made footwear for men and women in a warm Art Deco store opposite the fashion museum. His favourite brands include Céline, Martin Margiela MM6 and Megumi Ochi.

243 MONAR

The 5 best
JEWELLERY SHOPS

---

246 WOUTERS & HENDRIX
Lange Gasthuisstraat 13
Central Antwerp ①
+32 (0)3 218 54 45
www.wouters-hendrix.com

Katrin Wouters and Karen Hendrix have been selling their unique jewellery since they graduated from the Royal Academy of Fine Arts in 1984. They create beautiful rings and necklaces which they display in settings tinged with nostalgia. The contact page on their website is worth a click.

247 SALIMA THAKKER
Oever 28
Central Antwerp ①
+ 32 (0)3 237 37 49
www.salimathakker.com

A graduate of Antwerp's Royal Academy of Fine Arts, Salima Thakker sells beautiful, experimental jewellery in a small corner shop that once stocked Victor Sturm ceramic tiles. The black interior is decorated with purple orchids to create a romantic mood.

248 PASCALE MASSELIS
Zirkstraat 42
Central Antwerp ①
+32 (0)478 76 07 55
www.pascalemasselis.be

Pascale Masselis sells unique jewellery in a beautiful Parisian shop interior dating from 1885. The original shop stocked buttons in rows of tiny polished wooden drawers. It is now a nostalgic setting for Masselis' elaborate rings made from precious stones and gold thread.

249 WIM MEEUSSEN

Wijngaardstraat 11
Central Antwerp ①
+ 32 (0)3 232 19 13
www.wimmeeussen.be

Wim Meeussen sells his innovative gold jewellery in an elegant Art Nouveau shop near the Carolus Borromeuskerk. For the past 25 years, young couples have sat at the round table in the little back room to choose their wedding ring. Meeussen recently took over the Art Nouveau shop next door, painted the walls white, and started selling eccentric jewellery by modern designers, including inexpensive necklaces for children.

250 ANNE ZELLIEN

Kammenstraat 47
Central Antwerp ①
+32 (0)3 226 89 70
www.annezellien.be

Anne Zellien creates unique rings, earrings and pendants using silver, gold and precious stones. Some of her most striking pieces are inspired by the romantic jewellery of 17th and 18th century Europe. Her aim is to revive the tradition in which rings and necklaces were engraved with secret personal messages.

The 5 best shops for
ACCESSORIES

---

251 JULIJA'S SHOP

Nationalestraat 118
Central Antwerp ①
+32 (0)3 298 91 70
www.julijasshop.be

This shop has shelves lined with brightly-coloured knitting wool, stacks of the finest fabrics and boxes filled with every size of button. Julie and her colleagues are always pleased to explain the fine details of knitting a jumper or making a skirt from scratch.

252 BOON

Lombardenvest 2
Central Antwerp ①
+32 (0)3 232 33 87
www.glovesboon.be

This little shop has been selling gloves for over 120 years in a handsome interior lined with wooden drawers. The shop stocks a range of styles from simple black leather gloves to stylish zebra print.

253 ANNELIES TIMMERMANS

Aalmoezenierstraat 3
+32 (0)3 336 31 18
Central Antwerp ①
www.anneliestimmermans.
com

After studying graphic design and the art of leatherworking in Milan, Annelies Timmermans returned to Antwerp in 2008 to launch her own handbag collection. The bags are rather sober designs made by hand in a small Milan workshop.

254 BONAVENTURA

Aalmoezenierstraat 38
Central Antwerp ①

Here is a hidden shop with an authentic 1950s interior where you can find second-hand designer handbags by Chanel, Louis Vuitton or Delvaux. The owner Deborah Lodewijckx also sells vintage purses, bracelets and other nostalgic accessories.

255 EROTISCHE VERBEELDING

Kloosterstraat 165
Central Antwerp ①
+32 (0)3 226 89 50
www.erotischeverbeelding.be

Ann Cuyvers runs a sophisticated erotica shop aimed mainly at women. In contrast to the sleazy sex shops near the port, Erotische Verbeelding (Erotic Imagination) is decorated in a softly sensual boudoir style. This is the place to go for sensible advice on choosing lingerie, gadgets and accessories.

251 JULIJA'S SHOP

The 5 most stylish
DESIGN SHOPS

256 **ESPOO**
Vlaamse Kaai 57
Het Zuid ②
+32 (0)3 237 57 97
www.espoo.be

Dries Brys sells Nordic design in a store named after a small town in Finland. Passionate about cool brands like Hay, Muuto, Normann Copenhagen and Asplund, he has brought affordable contemporary design to Antwerp's southern docklands.

257 **REWIND**
Riemstraat 27
Het Zuid ②
+32 (0)3 296 71 96
www.rewinddesign.be

Stijn Gilles and Liesbet Wouters sell furniture made by European designers using recycled materials. Some of the ideas seem bizarre, like a table made out of old books or a chair created from recycled bottles. Not the cheapest way to furnish an apartment, but possibly the most original.

258 **MAGAZYN**
Steenhouwersvest 34
Central Antwerp ①
+32 (0)3 226 66 06
www.magazyn.be

Founded in 2008 by Thomas Haarmann, this minimalist design store moved in 2012 to a location close to the fashion museum. It stocks a small and carefully curated collection of ceramics, accessories and furniture. Most of the items are made by hand by craftsmen steeped in the old ways.

259 ATELIER SOLARSHOP

Dambruggestraat 48
Station Quarter ④
ateliersolarshop.blogspot.be

One of the most inspiring places in Antwerp, this store opposite the Winkelhaak design centre started as a pop-up initiative in an abandoned shop that once sold solar panels. It is now a permanent design shop where vintage furniture is displayed alongside edgy fashion. It also serves coffee and ices, and puts on the occasional concert.

260 HELDER

Vrijdagmarkt 13
Central Antwerp ①
+32 (0)3 289 43 18
www.studiohelder.be

Opened in 2010, this cool contemporary design shop is run by two designers, Diana Keller and Brecht Baert, who met while working for Ann Demeulemeester. As well as selling work by Sort of Coal, Chevalier Masson and Marijke de Cock, they create their own unique pieces.

258 MAGAZYN

COGELS-OSYLEI

20 BUILDINGS TO ADMIRE

The 5 most
IMPRESSIVE TOWERS

---

261 CATHEDRAL SPIRE
Handschoenmarkt
Central Antwerp ①

The north spire of Antwerp Cathedral slowly rose above the city's rooftops between 1420 and 1518. The architect designed the upper sections in a beautiful Brabant gothic style, creating the tallest spire in the Low Countries, at 123 metres. Concerts are played on the carillon in the tower every Sunday, from May to September, from 3 pm to 4 pm. You can also catch evening concerts in July and August, on Mondays from 8 pm to 9 pm.

262 KBC BANK TOWER
Eiermarkt 20
Central Antwerp ①

Built from 1929 to 1932, the KBC bank tower was Europe's first skyscraper, constructed like the skyscrapers of Manhattan around a steel skeleton. Designed in Art Deco style, the tower was originally 87.5 metres high, but gained an additional 10 metres in 1976.

261 **CATHEDRAL**

262 **KBC BANK TOWER**

263 **OUDAAN POLICE TOWER**
Oudaan 5
Central Antwerp ①

The brutal grey concrete tower looming over Antwerp's fashion district was built in the 1960s by the Belgian modernist Renaat Braem. Some people love it. Others find it an eyesore. It is now occupied by Antwerp's police headquarters. You can visit the 12th floor, but only by booking a group tour.

264 **DEN BELL**
Francis Wellesplein 1
Southern Antwerp ⑦
+32 (0)3 221 13 33

Originally built for the Bell Telephone Company in 1958, this is a striking example of Belgian modernism. Now this 12-floor building houses the city administration. The interior is worth a glance, especially to see the spectacular curved staircase that rises through the building.

265 **PAGADDER TOWER**
Hofstraat 15
Central Antwerp ①

The tall brick tower that rises above the old stock exchange building dates from the 16th century. Originally a lookout tower, it takes its name from the *pagadders*, or children, who were sent to the top to spot ships arriving in port.

The 5 most striking
MODERN BUILDINGS

---

266 BRAEM PAVILION
Middelheimlaan 61
Suburbs (Middelheim) ⑫
+32 (0)3 288 33 60
www.middelheimmuseum.be

Renaat Braem, a student of Le Corbusier, built a small architectural gem in the Middelheim sculpture museum park in 1971. Designed to display fragile sculptures, this neat white building is composed of sensual curved forms.

267 DE SINGEL
Desguinlei 25
Southern Antwerp ⑦
+32 (0)3 248 28 28
www.desingel.be

Built by Léon Stynen in the 1960s, De Singel is a bold modern building next to the ring motorway. Originally a concert hall and music conservatory, it now includes an architecture institute located in the wood-clad extension designed by Stéphane Beel in 2011. The strange organic forms combined with the airy transparency make this an intriguing building.

268 LAW COURTS
Bolivarplaats
Het Zuid ②

Completed in 2006, the new law courts on the southern edge of the city were designed by the Richard Rogers Partnership. The pointed roofs that rise above the individual courtrooms were intended to suggest ships' sails or church spires, but locals prefer to see them as upturned frites cones.

269 **VAN ROOSMALEN HOUSE**
Goede Hoopstraat/
Sint Michielskaai
Central Antwerp ①

This striking black-and-white striped corner building was designed by the architect Bob Van Reeth in 1985. Built as a private home for the interior designer Will Van Roosmalen, it was the first contemporary building on the Scheldt waterfront, based on an unrealised project by Adolf Loos for Josephine Baker.

270 **WESTKAAI**
Kattendijkdok-
Westkaai
Het Eilandje ⑧

A row of apartment blocks designed by Swiss architects Diener & Diener has brought sober contemporary design to Het Eilandje district. The project involves the construction of six elegant towers, each 16 floors high, in slightly different styles.

268 LAW COURTS

The 5 finest
ART NOUVEAU
buildings

---

271 **HET BOOTJE**
  Schildersstraat 2
  Het Zuid ②

The architect F. Smet-Verhas designed this striking Art Nouveau house behind the Royal Fine Arts Museum in 1901. It is called Het Bootje, the Little Boat, because of the corner balcony shaped like a ship's prow. The elaborate iron lamp under the balcony adds a further touch of eccentricity.

272 **STEINER SCHOOL**
  Volkstraat 40
  Het Zuid ②

This spectacular Art Nouveau building was built for the socialist party in 1901. The flamboyant building is decorated with distinctive Art Nouveau arched windows, elaborate ironwork and carved figures at the top. It is now occupied by a Rudolf Steiner school.

273 **ROTTERDAMSTRAAT 53-55**
  Rotterdamstraat 53-55
  Antwerpen-Noord ⑨

This striking house was built in 1912 by the architect Jos Goeyvaerts in a strange style that blends Art Nouveau and Egyptian motifs. The decoration reflects Masonic ideas that were circulating in Belgium at the time.

274 **MERCATORSTRAAT 102-106**

Mercatorstraat 102-106
Jewish Quarter ⑤

Facing the railway viaduct, this set of three Art Nouveau houses with yellow brick façades and wrought iron balconies was built in 1901 by Emiel van Averbeke. The same architect also designed the Art Nouveau Steiner School, the Art Deco Veldstraat swimming pool and the KBC Tower.

275 **RUYS**

Sint-Jorispoort 26
Central Antwerp ①
+32 (0)3 232 49 65

The most beautiful Art Nouveau shop in Antwerp dates from 1902 when the jeweller Albert Ruys transformed the family shop where his father had started as a silversmith in 1854. The new building, three houses wide, has a beautiful Art Nouveau facade, mosaic floors, carved wood display cabinets and soft lighting.

271 HET BOOTJE

The 5 most striking buildings in the
ZURENBORG QUARTER

---

276 THE FOUR SEASONS
Generaal van
Merlenstraat 27-30
Zurenborg ⑥

The architect Joseph Bascourt designed these four corner houses in the 1890s. The seasons are identified by gilded mosaics on the walls bearing the words *Herfst*, *Winter*, *Lente* and *Zomer*. Each season has its own symbolic plants and flowers, such as vines for autumn, roses for summer and holly to represent winter.

277 THE SUNFLOWER
Cogels-Osylei 50
Zurenborg ⑥

This striking white Art Nouveau house takes its name from the gilded sunflowers that decorate the façade. The architect Jules Hofman carved a stone with his signature just below the balcony. The house next door continues the floral theme with a tall wrought iron tulip on top, while No. 44 is identified by an iris.

278 DE WITTE PALEIZEN
Cogels-Osylei
Zurenborg ⑥

A group of four impressive buildings overlooks a small roundabout on Cogels-Osylei. The buildings – each containing three family homes – were apparently inspired by the Château de Chambord on the Loire.

279 **THE BATTLE OF WATERLOO**

Waterloostraat 11
Zurenborg ⑥

An Art Nouveau house named *De Slag van Waterloo* is decorated with the distinctive silhouettes of Wellington and Napoleon. Another house in the same street is decorated with glazed ceramic panels depicting scenes from the 1815 battle fought just south of Brussels.

280 **COGELS-OSYLEI 80**

Cogels-Osylei 80
Zurenborg ⑥

Half hidden by trees, this beautiful Art Nouveau house has a spectacular stone staircase that sweeps up to the porch. The house is an almost exact copy of an Art Nouveau building in Brussels.

280 COGELS-OSYLEI 80

277 THE SUNFLOWER

MAS PANORAMA

75 PLACES TO DISCOVER ANTWERP

The 5 most
IMPRESSIVE VIEWS

---

281 **LEFT BANK**
Sint-Jansvliet
Central Antwerp ①

It takes about ten minutes to walk through the Sint Anna tunnel to reach the left bank, where there is a small park and some benches on the waterfront. Artists have been coming here since the 15th century to paint panoramic views of the city, including Jan Baptist Bonnecroy's *View of Antwerp* of 1658 that now hangs in the MAS museum.

282 **MAS ROOFTOP PANORAMA**
Hanzestedenplaats 1
Het Eilandje ⑧
+ 32 (0)3 338 44 34
www.mas.be

Opened in 2012, the MAS museum has a 10th floor roof terrace that offers spectacular views of the old town and the port area. The terrace can be visited free, Tuesday to Sunday, from 9.00 to 23.30. One of the best times to be here is just before sunset.

283 **RED STAR LINE OBSERVATION TOWER**
Montevideostraat 3
Het Eilandje ⑧
www.redstarline.be

Here is a new tower offering a different view of the city. The 30-metre structure, designed to look like a ship's funnel, rises above the old Red Star Line sheds, where emigrants boarded ships bound for New York. Completed in 2012, the tower forms part of the Red Star Line Museum.

284 M KHAFE

Leuvenstraat 32
Het Zuid ②
+32 (0)3 260 99 99
www.muhka.be

Here is a secret rooftop terrace hidden at the top of a grain silo. It can be reached by a side door to the left of the main entrance of M HKA, the museum of contemporary art. Here you get unexpected views of warehouses, loft apartments and the occasional cruise ship.

285 LANGE RIDDERSSTRAAT

Lange Riddersstraat 24
Central Antwerp ①

One of the best views of the Cathedral spire comes as you walk down Lange Ridderstraat. Stand next to No. 24 and you see the Gothic spire in the distance framed by brick gabled houses. Continue to Pelgrimstraat for another spectacular view.

281 LEFT BANK

The 5 most
INSPIRING MUSEUMS

---

286 **MOMU**
Nationalestraat 28
Central Antwerp ①
+32 (0)3 470 27 70
www.momu.be

The fashion museum MoMu occupies a grand 19th century building renovated in 1999 by Marie-José Van Hee. The architect has added a spacious lobby and a monumental staircase made from resilient merbau wood. As well as the fashion museum, the building is home to the Flanders Fashion Institute.

287 **FOMU**
Waalse Kaai 47
Het Zuid ②
+32 (0)3 242 93 00
www.fotomuseum.be

Once a warehouse, now a photography museum where you can see works by some of the world's greatest photographers. The film museum and Café UFO are in the same building, while the museum shop is a good place to browse for books, postcards and vintage cameras.

288 **VLEESHUIS**
Vleeshouwersstraat 38
Central Antwerp ①
+32 (0)3 233 64 04
www.museumvleeshuis.be

An inspiring museum of musical instruments where you wander around with a digital player and headphones listening to strange instruments from the past. You might hear bagpipe music from the time of Bruegel or a virginal built in an Antwerp workshop.

289 **PANAMARENKO HOUSE**

Biekorfstraat 2
Antwerpen-Noord ⑨
www.muhka.be

The strange helipad on the roof identifies Panamarenko's house. The Antwerp artist lived here for more than 30 years along with his mother, a parrot and a collection of aircraft parts. Panamarenko builds unlikely mechanical flying machines and imaginary birds.

290 **DE POORTERSWONING**

Pelgrimstraat 15
Central Antwerp ①
+32 (0)3 234 08 09
www.pelgrom.be

The mediaeval beer cellar *De Pelgrom* is hardly a secret, but the private museum upstairs is barely known. Here you find rooms furnished in 15th-century style with old cooking pots and a caged parrot. The owner offers a lively guided tour. Open Saturdays and Sundays from 12.00 to 18.30.

The 5 most
SECRET STREETS

---

291 **VLAEYKENSGANG**
Oudekoornmarkt 16/
Pelgrimstraat 8
Central Antwerp ①

A narrow passage leads into a network of crooked lanes, small cobbled courtyards and 16th century whitewashed houses. This quarter had become a slum by the 1960s, but the antique dealer Axel Vervoordt bought up the houses and restored them as restaurants and art galleries.

292 **MAESGANCK**
Korte Ridderstraat 23
Central Antwerp ①

A forgotten alley lies hidden behind an antique dealer's shop in the Sint Andries quarter. The 16th century houses, which can be glimpsed through a metal screen, once belonged to an almshouse called Godshuis Maesganck. The buildings were restored by the antique dealer in the 1970s.

293 **PAARDEKENSGANG**
Willem Lepelstraat 14
Central Antwerp ①

An old gate decorated with a horse's head leads into a hidden alley with whitewashed houses and potted plants. This lane used to be notorious for its rowdy cafés and brothels. Now you barely hear a sound.

294 KORTE BRILSTRAAT

Korte Brilstraat
University Quarter ③

This dark cobbled lane off the Stadswaag is one of the most authentic streets left in the old port quarter. It is lined with ancient brick warehouses that have been turned into offices and apartments.

295 RIJKE BEUKELAERSTRAAT

Rijke Beukelaerstraat
Central Antwerp ①

An attractive lane of 17th century houses in the Sint Andries quarter where cars are banned and residents sit out on the street. The garage door at No. 7 has been painted with a trompe l'oeil showing an imaginary lane called Gazettesteeg.

291 VLAEYKENSGANG

The 5 most
STRIKING BUILDINGS

296 **CENTRAAL STATION**
Astridplein
Station Quarter ④

Built in 1905 by the architect Louis Delacenserie, Antwerp's main railway station is considered to be one of the most beautiful stations in the world. It has a high domed booking hall, a sweeping iron and glass canopy above the tracks and a viaduct decorated with turrets.

297 **RUBENSHUIS**
Wapperplein 9
Central Antwerp ①
+32 (0)3 201 15 55
www.rubenshuis.be

The family home of Antwerp's most famous citizen was modelled on an Italian palazzo. It's an impressive baroque building with a huge studio where Rubens would show paintings to clients. But the most seductive spot is the garden hidden at the back.

298 **DE WINKELHAAK**
Lange Winkelhaakstraat 26
Station Quarter ④
+32 (0)3 727 10 30
www.winkelhaak.be

Launched in 2002, the Winkelhaak design centre has injected new life into a run-down neighbourhood near the main station. The interior is friendly and colourful, with the design shop *100 gr Design* located on the ground floor and the co-working space Bar d'Office down in the basement.

299 PLANTIN MORETUS MUSEUM

Vrijdagmarkt 22-23
Central Antwerp ⓘ
+32 (0)3 221 14 50
www.museumplantin-moretus.be

The rooms of this beautiful Renaissance building are filled with relics of the Plantin-Moretus publishing house, including cases of lead type, old books and detailed maps. One of Europe's most beautiful museums, it tells the story of printing at a time when Antwerp was at the heart of the global economy.

300 STADHUIS

Grote Markt 1
Central Antwerp ⓘ

The massive Renaissance town hall designed by Cornelis Floris has dominated the Grote Markt since it was completed in 1565. The interior conceals marvels that few ever see, including the *Schoon Verdiep*, or bel étage, where the mayor has an office.

The 5 best
TRAM RIDES

301 **TRAM 10**
Astridplein
Station Quarter ④

The old-fashioned trams on line 10 follow a circular route through the old town, down narrow cobbled streets where they can barely squeeze through. From Centraal Station, the tram goes down Lange Nieuwstraat and across the lively Melkmarkt before turning back to the station. Pick a quiet time of day to avoid the crush.

302 **TRAM 11**
Astridplein
Station Quarter ④

The tram runs from Astridplein in the direction of Melkmarkt. Back at Astridplein, it continues down a street behind the zoo and heads south to Zurenborg, passing the attractive squares Draakplaats and Tramplaats on the way. But the best part of the ride comes towards the end as the tram rumbles down Cogels-Osylei, past some of the most flamboyant buildings in the city.

303 **TRAM 7**

Mechelseplein
Central Antwerp ①
Zurenborg ⑥

This is a useful tram to get to MAS. The route runs from the southern suburbs to the edge of the harbour district, passing along broad streets lined with fashion boutiques and through cobbled squares filled with café terraces. Look out for the white De Koninck brewery as the tram heads south.

304 **TRAM 12**

Astridplein
Station Quarter ④

Tram 12 follows an interesting route from Centraal Station to Groenplaats, past some impressive buildings, including the opera house, National Bank, the new law courts, the Royal Fine Arts Museum and the Tropical Institute.

305 **TRAM 4**

Burgemeester
Ryckaertsplein 1
Jewish Quarter ⑤

Tram 4 passes through central Antwerp along several streets lined with fashion boutiques. Pick it up at Berchem Station in the direction of Hoboken. This route goes down Lange Leemstraat, which has a strong Jewish identity, and past the Mechelseplein, which is filled with café terraces in summer. But the best part of the ride comes as the tram slowly circles the imposing Free Scheldt monument.

The 5 most

UNUSUAL BUILDINGS

---

306 SINT-ANNA TUNNEL

Sint Jansvliet
Central Antwerp ①

The 572-metre white-tiled pedestrian tunnel under the River Scheldt was built in 1933 to connect the left bank with the old town. The entrance is reached by an Art Deco brick building which contains the original wooden escalators. Allow ten minutes to walk to the other side.

307 ST FELIXPAKHUIS

Oudeleeuwenrui 29
Het Eilandje ⑧
+ 32 (0)3 338 94 11
www.felixarchief.be
www.felixpakhuis.nu

An impressive covered street runs through the middle of the massive St Felix Warehouse. It was created as a fire-break in 1861 after fire swept through the enormous building. The warehouse – once used for storing coffee, cheese and tobacco – lay abandoned for many years, but was restored in 2006. It now contains the city archives, an exhibition space and several restaurants.

308 HANDELSBEURS

Borzestraat
Central Antwerp ①

The original building from 1531 was destroyed by fire, but the city replaced it with a fairly faithful replica. Now the Handelsbeurs is being restored to create 'the most beautiful event venue in Belgium,' while an adjoining building will become a luxury hotel.

309 VILLA TINTO

Verversrui 17
University Quarter ③
www.villat.be

This could well be the world's most unusual brothel. With its bold red walls, it looks more like a modern office block. It aims to provide a safe working environment for some 100 women involved in the sex trade. As well as little cubicles for sex workers, the building incorporates a police station, doctor's surgery and a bed and breakfast.

310 ELEPHANT HOUSE

Koningin Astridplein 26
Station Quarter ④
+32 (0)3 202 45 40
www.zooantwerpen.be

Founded in 1843, the Antwerp zoo has several eccentric buildings where animals are kept. The most fanciful is the Elephant House, constructed in 1856 and decorated with hieroglyphics composed by a local Egyptologist, who included a declaration in praise of 'King Léopold I, Sun and Life of Belgium.'

306 SINT-ANNA TUNNEL

The 5 best
CARTOON MURALS

---

311 JAN BOSSCHAERT
Wolstraat 12
Central Antwerp ①

A wall in the narrow Moriaanstraatje (Moor Lane) is decorated with a cartoon mural based on the work of comic strip artist Jan Bosschaert. It shows the statue of the Flemish writer Hendrik Conscience on the nearby Conscienceplein with a heap of miscellaneous books scattered on the ground.

312 MERHO
Paradijsstraat 4
University Quarter ③

Turn down the little lane called Paradijsstraat and you will find a comic mural covering the entire side wall of a house. This work from 2007 is based on the *Kiekeboe* series by the graphic artist Merho. The mural includes an imaginary lane leading off the Paradijsstraat.

313 JAN VAN DER VEKEN
Eiermarkt 8
Central Antwerp ①

This mural on a blank back wall of the KBC Bank was created by Jan van der Veken, a comic book illustrator from Ghent whose work has appeared on the cover of *The New Yorker*. Van der Veken's affectionate portrait of city life reflects the Atomic Style of the 1960s.

314 **DICK MATENA**
Korte Nieuwstraat
Central Antwerp ①

A striking 2008 comic mural based on a graphic novel by Dick Matena appears outside the Hendrik Conscience Library. It shows Frans Laarmans, the failed capitalist in Willem Elsschot's novella *Kaas* (Cheese), striding across Grote Markt with a bag full of unsold Edam cheese.

315 **ILAH**
Opposite Keizerstraat 58
University Quarter ③

The illustrator Ilah is famous for simple comic strips in *De Morgen* newspaper featuring a young woman called Cordelia. The mural in Keizerstraat, commissioned by the university, shows Cordelia struggling with her studies.

313 **MURAL BY JAN VAN DER VEKEN**

The 5 best places to find
ANTWERP PAINTINGS

316 **ROCKOXHUIS**
Keizerstraat 12
University Quarter ③
+32 (0)3 201 92 50
www.rockoxhuis.be

With the Royal Fine Arts Museum closed for renovation work until 2017, many of the paintings have moved to new locations such as the Rockoxhuis, where Flemish Masters have been hung in the 17th century rooms to recreate the mood of an Antwerp cabinet of curiosities. Here is where you now find works by Jan van Eyck, Rogier van der Weyden and Hans Memling.

317 **KONINGIN FABIOLAZAAL**
Jezusstraat 28
Central Antwerp ①
+32 (0)3 203 42 04

Located in the provincial safety institute, the Queen Fabiola Hall displays paintings from the Royal Fine Arts Museum's 20th century collection. The building has a striking 1970s façade decorated with a health and safety frieze illustrating accidents in the workplace.

318 ONZE-LIEVE-VROUWE-KATHEDRAAL

Handschoenmarkt
Central Antwerp ①

Eight heavy wooden altarpieces which normally hang in the Royal Fine Arts Museum have been moved back to the Cathedral where they originally hung. The works will remain in the Cathedral until 2017 alongside Rubens' two masterpieces, the *Raising of the Cross* and the *Descent from the Cross*.

319 MAYER VAN DEN BERGH

Lange Gasthuisstraat 19
Central Antwerp ①
+32 (0)3 338 81 88
www.mayervandenbergh.be

Located in a dark neo-Gothic house, this remarkable museum looks a bit forbidding. Overcome your caution and you will discover one of the finest private art collections in Europe. It includes mediaeval manuscripts, sculpture and prints, but the highlight is Pieter Bruegel's *Dulle Griet*.

320 SINT PAULUSKERK

Veemarkt 13
Central Antwerp ①
+32 (0)3 232 32 67

The church is hard to find. It may not even be open when you do track it down. But it is worth making an effort as this beautiful baroque building contains a series of paintings by Antwerp artists such as Rubens, Van Dyck and Jordaens.

The 5 best
VIRGIN MARY
statues

---

321 OUDE KOORNMARKT
Oude Koornmarkt 32
Central Antwerp ①

A fanatical devotion to the Virgin Mary developed in Antwerp under Spanish rule in the 17th century. Intended as a counterblast to the Protestant revolt in the north, the cult led to the beautiful statues of the Virgin and Child you see on many buildings. One of the most striking examples can be seen at the end of the Pelgrimstraat.

322 VLASMARKT
Vlasmarkt 36
Central Antwerp ①

Wearing a red dress and blue cape, this statue of the Virgin holds Jesus while a green snake slithers around her feet. She is protected from the rain by a green canopy hung with seven bells, and the sculpture is lit at night by an elaborate street lamp decorated with more bells.

323 STEENHOUWERSVEST
Steenhouwersvest 22
Central Antwerp ①

On a corner near the Plantin-Moretus Museum, this statue of the Virgin and Child stands on a base surrounded by three angels' heads. A simple grey canopy keeps off the rain.

324 **WOLSTRAAT**

Wolstraat 23
Central Antwerp ①

Attached to a house corner opposite De Kat café, this slender Madonna holds a Child wearing a gold crown. The figures are sheltered by a wooden arch painted blue with a beautiful gilded sunburst above.

325 **KEIZERSTRAAT**

Keizerstraat 73
University Quarter ③

This beautiful baroque statue of the Virgin was carved for a chapel in the Keizerstraat that was later demolished. The Virgin, in flowing robes, stands on a blue globe with a serpent at her feet, while two angels float at her side.

321 **OUDE KOORNMARKT**

The 5 most interesting
NEIGHBOURHOODS

326 **HET EILANDJE**
Bonapartedok
Het Eilandje ⑧

The docklands district to the north of the old city is an area of stone quays, brick warehouses and deep docks. Known as Het Eilandje (the little island) it fell into decline in the 20th century but has emerged in recent years as a cool urban neighbourhood of new museums, loft apartments, waterfront cafés and design shops.

327 **SINT ANDRIES**
Kloosterstraat
Central Antwerp ①

This was once one of the poorest parts of the old city, but the quarter around the Sint Andrieskerk has been transformed in recent years. The most exciting developments have happened along Kloosterstraat, once a street of junk shops but now lined with design stores, cool cafés and antique shops.

328 SCHIPPERSKWARTIER

Falconplein
University Quarter ③

The Schipperskwartier was once the red light district, but the city has cleaned up much of the neighbourhood and built a high-tech official brothel called Villa Tinto. A few seedy bars and sex shops have survived, but they are gradually giving way to loft apartments, co-working bars and cool B&Bs.

329 BORGERHOUT

Borgerhout ⑩

Van Gogh spent a few miserable months living in this district behind Centraal Station. It is still a popular neighbourhood for young artists and writers, but also for immigrants from Turkey, Morocco and Afghanistan. The restored Roma cinema shows that it is on the way up again.

330 DIAMOND QUARTER

Hoveniersstraat
Station Quarter ④

Antwerp's diamond quarter occupies a warren of narrow streets and alleys near Centraal Station. It is hard to imagine anywhere less glamorous, less sparkling, than this drab area of concrete office blocks and police checkpoints, yet a large part of the world's diamond trade is concentrated in this area.

The 5 best places to spot
STREET ART

331 KOPSTRAATJE

Kopstraatje
Central Antwerp ①

Until 2012 this was a dingy alley off the Kammenstraat. Then the Antwerp graffiti artist Steve Locatelli invited 14 international friends to come with their spray cans and liven up the walls. You find some striking street art here, but the alley is still a bit dingy.

332 PARK SPOOR NOORD

Viaduct Dam
Asiadok Zuidkaai
Antwerpen-Noord ⑨

During the 2009 graffiti festival *Can It*, several graffiti artists sprayed street art in the dark underpass below the motorway in Park Spoor Noord. You can admire striking art here by the Aerosol Kings collective.

333 VINCENT VAN GOGH-PLEIN

Vincent van Goghplein
Duinstraat
Antwerpen-Noord ⑨

Copies of famous Van Gogh works were painted by local students on a blank wall in the Stuivenberg district. They commemorate Van Gogh's stay in Antwerp in 1885-86, when he studied at the Royal Academy. He told his brother Theo that Antwerp was "very curious and beautiful for an artist" and the women were "really exceptionally beautiful".

334 LUX

Sint Aldegondiskaai 20
Het Eilandje ⑧

Look out for the mural with scenes of decadent nightlife next to Lux restaurant. Painted on a wooden hoarding by the Antwerp artist Jan Scheirs, it recalls 1930s German Expressionism. But it will disappear one day when the empty building site beside Lux is developed.

335 BERCHEM STATION

Burgemeester
Ryckaertsplein 1
Zurenborg ⑥

A long wall running along platform 7 at Berchem station is covered with graffiti art on the theme of mobility. The project was organised in 2012 by Big Uncle Graffiti Team to encourage creative graffiti art.

331 KOPSTRAATJE

The 5 most romantic
SECRET GARDENS

---

336 **BEGIJNHOF**
Rodestraat 41
University Quarter ③

Hidden behind a high brick wall is one of the most secret gardens in Antwerp. It belongs to the *Begijnhof*, a secluded religious community of red-brick houses and cobbled lanes established for single women in 1544.

337 **PLANTIN MORETUS GARDEN**
Vrijdagmarkt 22-23
Central Antwerp ①
+32 (0)3 221 14 50
www.museumplantin-moretus.be

Here is a beautiful Renaissance garden hidden within the walls of the Plantin Moretus Museum. Created in 1639 by Balthasar Moretus the Elder, it is modelled on an Italian formal garden. A smaller, more secret garden was added behind the museum shop in 2002.

338 **ST PAULUSKERK**
Sint-Paulusstraat 20
Central Antwerp ①

A grand neoclassical coach entrance leads into a forgotten garden behind the Sint Pauluskerk. Not many people know about this mysterious spot where you find an overgrown ruin, Lourdes grotto and a 'monument to the unknown refugee' created in 2005.

339 ANTWERP ACADEMY GARDEN

Mutsaardstraat 31
University Quarter ③

The art school where Van Gogh briefly studied in 1886 overlooks a mysterious, overgrown garden filled with crumbling stone statues and architectural fragments. This rather romantic spot is sometimes the setting for intriguing student art installations.

340 BOTANICAL GARDEN

Leopoldstraat 24
Central Antwerp ①
+32 (0)3 232 40 87

The small botanical garden on Leopoldstraat was originally planted as a medicinal herb garden. It is now a romantic place with meandering paths, rocky outcrops and hidden benches. The former gardener's cottage is now a restaurant.

336 BEGIJNHOF

The 5 most attractive
SMALL SQUARES

---

341 HENDRIK CONSCIENCE-PLEIN

Hendrik Conscience-plein
Central Antwerp ①

Named after the 19th century Flemish writer Hendrik Conscience, this beautiful square is dominated by the baroque Carolus Borromeuskerk and the old city library. It became the first car-free square in Antwerp in 1968 after some local artists closed it off with blocks of industrial ice.

342 DRAAKPLAATS

Draakplaats
Zurenborg ⑥

A roundabout on the edge of the Zurenborg district is bisected by a railway viaduct and crossed by tram lines. The cafés on the square have pavement terraces where you can sit on summer evenings while goods trains rumble overhead deep into the night, adding to the somewhat surreal mood.

343 STADSWAAG

Stadswaag
University Quarter ③

This cobbled square planted with old trees was once the site of the city's weigh house. Surrounded by old brick warehouses, it is a sleepy, forgotten spot during the day, but the square slowly comes to life in the evening as the bars open their doors.

344 DAGERAADPLAATS
Dageraadplaats
Zurenborg ⑥

This inviting urban square is surrounded by shops, cafés and restaurants. You can watch a basketball game, kick around a football or sit on the terrace of Zeezicht with a glass of La Chouffe. It is worth dropping by after dark to see the artificial starry night created using a network of suspended lights.

345 OSSENMARKT
Ossenmarkt
University Quarter ③

This little square can easily be spotted on old maps of Antwerp. You just need to look for the cows, for this was once a cattle market on the edge of the old town. It is now a square with popular cafés where students meet after classes.

345 OSSENMARKT

The 5 most secret
CHURCHES

---

346 SINT CAROLUS BORROMEUSKERK

Hendrik Conscience-plein

Central Antwerp ①

Rubens is believed to have designed the baroque façade of the Sint Carolus Borromeuskerk. He certainly painted the ceiling inside. The façade is a gorgeous composition crowded with cherubs and pediments, but Rubens' ceiling was destroyed in a fire.

347 ELZENVELD

Lange Gasthuisstraat 45

Central Antwerp ①

www.elzenveld.be

Not many people know about this 15th century Gothic hospital and chapel. The entrance lies down a narrow cobbled lane near the botanical gardens. Once through the gate, you find yourself in a secret garden. Go through the main entrance and turn left at the cloakrooms to find the hidden chapel.

348 KAPEL VAN ONZE-LIEVE-VROUW-TOEVLUCHT

Schoenmarkt 8

Central Antwerp ①

Guidebooks don't mention this tiny brick chapel dating from 1477, yet it is a memorable place filled with marble plaques, tiny red candles and masses of fresh flowers. It is sometimes called the prostitutes' chapel because women came from the red light district to pray here.

349 KERKSCHIP

Houtdok
Het Eilandje ⑧
www.kerkschip-antwerpen.be

The St Joseph Church occupies a strange concrete ship built in Rotterdam in the Second World War to supply German U-boats. It was turned into a seamen's church and social centre in 1950 and moored in a remote area of the port. Recently moved to a dock at Het Eilandje, it contains a chapel, meeting hall and barge museum.

350 OOSTERWEELKERK

Oosterweelsesteenweg
Suburbs (Port) ⑫

A solitary 18th century stone church lies in a hollow surrounded by petroleum installations and shipping containers. The church is all that remains of the village of Oosterweel, which was erased from the map during the expansion of the port in 1929. The building is closed and inaccessible, the last sad relic of a vanished community.

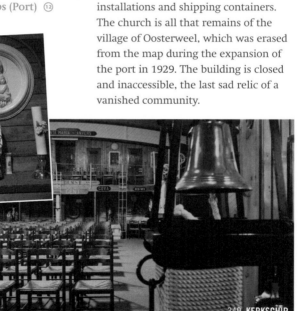

349 KERKSCHIP

The 5 most
SECRET COURTYARDS

---

351 MOUNT CALVARY
Sint Pauluskerk
Central Antwerp ①

This bizarre religious garden hidden behind the Sint Pauluskerk contains a fake mountain and 63 baroque statues telling the story of the Crucifixion. Two Dominican friars worked for half a century, from 1697 to 1747, to create this folly, which the French poet Baudelaire dismissed as "ridiculous".

352 OUDE BEURS
Hofstraat 15
Central Antwerp ①

The world's oldest stock exchange building is hidden behind a white neoclassical building. Go through the entrance and you find yourself in a cobbled courtyard enclosed by gothic arcades. This is where merchants gathered in the 16th century to strike deals.

353 HOF VAN LIERE
Venusstraat 25
University Quarter ③

The Hof van Liere now belongs to the university, but this late gothic palace was originally the home of the Antwerp burgomaster Aert van Liere. It was praised by Albrecht Dürer. The building was later occupied by English Merchant Adventurers before it became a Jesuit college.

354 SINT NICOLAASPLAATS

Lange Nieuwstraat 3
University Quarter ③

It's easy to miss this hidden cobbled courtyard named after the statue of St Nicholas standing in the middle. The 17th century brick buildings were restored by Fred Van Averbeke in 1958-68 and the little Gothic chapel in the corner became home to the Royal Van Campen Puppet Theatre.

355 MERCATOR ORTELIUS-HUIS

Kloosterstraat 15
Central Antwerp ①

Most people have never seen the courtyard inside the 16th century palace known as the Mercator-Orteliushuis. Until recently the building was occupied by the city archaeology department, but it is now being rented out to small businesses including a stylish wine bar. Worth a look inside if it is open.

352 OUDE BEURS

20 PLACES
FOR CULTURE

———

The 5 most inspiring
ART GALLERIES

---

356 **ZENO X**
Godtsstraat 15
Borgerhout ⑩
+32 (0)3 216 38 88
www.zeno-x.com

The famous Zeno X gallery recently moved from Het Zuid to a converted industrial building in Borgerhout. Run by Frank Demaegd, it exhibits works by Belgian painters like Luc Tuymans, Michael Borremans and Dirk Braeckman. Opening nights are always packed.

357 **DE ZWARTE PANTER**
Hoogstraat 70
Central Antwerp ①
+32 (0)3 233 13 45
www.dezwartepanter.com

A sculpture of a black panther above a Gothic doorway marks the entrance to this gallery established in 1970. The art is displayed in a warren of buildings that once belonged to a mediaeval hospital. The Antwerp artist Fred Bervoets regularly exhibits his enormous expressionist paintings here.

358 **TIM VAN LAERE**
Verlatstraat 23-25
Het Zuid ②
+32 (0)3 257 14 17
www.timvanlaeregallery.com

Tim Van Laere's bright, white-walled gallery has hosted some inspiring exhibitions by international artists like Edward Lipski and Ed Templeton. Van Laere always attracts a big crowd during the monthly Nocturnes when Antwerp galleries stay open until 9 pm.

359 EXTRA CITY

Tulpstraat 79
Antwerpen-Noord ⑨
+32 (0)3 677 16 55
www.extracity.org

This experimental art centre started out in a condemned building in the harbour area, then moved to an old industrial ruin in North Antwerp. Expect to be challenged by the art, and even by the building. A dodgy iron staircase leads to the entrance, and exhibitions are held in cold loft spaces.

360 FIFTY ONE FINE ART PHOTOGRAPHY

Zirkstraat 20
Central Antwerp ①
+32 (0)3 289 84 58
www.gallery51.com

Gallery owner Roger Szmulewicz devotes his striking white exhibition space to Belgian and international photography. Ranked as one of the ten best photo galleries in the world, it exhibits classic American photographers such as Andre Kertesz and Saul Leiter as well as contemporary European, Japanese and African photographers.

The 5 best places to
WATCH A FILM

---

361 **DE ROMA**
Turnhoutsebaan 286
Borgerhout ⑩
+32 (0)3 292 97 40
www.deroma.be

This old cinema was built in 1927 and might have vanished, like so many others, but it was saved by locals, who restored it as a film house and concert venue. The nostalgic interior is decorated with film posters from the early days of cinema along with photographs of the Antwerp cyclist Stan Ockers.

362 **FILMHUIS KLAPPEI**
Klappeistraat 2
Antwerpen-Noord ⑨
+32 (0)3 272 51 10
www.klappei.be

This small filmhouse occupies a Flemish gabled building, constructed in 1916 as a police station. It still has the original prison cells, but it has been renovated to incorporate a 50-seat cinema and café. The programme includes some inspired ideas, like a season of architecture films or a Kinky Klappei evening devoted to soft porn movies.

363 **CARTOON'S**
Kaasstraat 4
Central Antwerp ①
+32 (0)3 232 96 32
www.cartoons-cinema.be

Here is an authentic three-screen cinema in a quiet street near the Scheldt. You buy the ticket at a little box office outside and settle into a snug cinema. The programme leans towards international arthouse movies.

364 **CINEMA ZUID**

Lakenstraat 14
Het Zuid ②
+32 (0)3 242 93 57
www.cinemazuid.be

The film house Cinema Zuid offers the most adventurous film programme in Antwerp. They might be screening a classic horror film from 1920s Berlin in one room and a recent indie movie in the other. Located in the same building as the photography museum.

365 **KAVKA**

Oudaan 14
Central Antwerp ①
+32 (0)3 290 88 17
www.kavka.be

A 19th century coach gate near the police tower leads into a courtyard with graffiti-covered walls. This abandoned site has been turned into an edgy youth centre. As well as organising concerts and art exhibitions, Kavka occasionally screens alternative films.

364 **CINEMA ZUID**

The 5 most surprising sculptures in
MIDDELHEIM PARK

—————

366 **MISCONCEIVABLE**
Kasteel Middelheim
Suburbs (Middelheim) ⑬

Erwin Wurm's humourous art works are dotted around Middelheim Park. His most striking work, *Misconceivable*, features an astonishing bent yacht resting on a brick wall. The same artist is responsible for the crashed car leaning against Carl Milles' 1949 sculpture *Pegasus*.

367 **ARCHAEOPTERIX LITHOGRAFICA**
Middelheim Park
Suburbs (Middelheim) ⑬

The Antwerp artist Panamarenko has spent a lifetime creating odd flying machines and prehistoric birds. His tiny mechanical bird *Archaeopterix Lithografica* sits on top of a dead tree, flapping its wings helplessly when anyone approaches.

368 **ROMAN STREET**
Middelheim Park
Suburbs (Middelheim) ⑬

Guillaume Bijl's *Roman Street* lies hidden in the woods. It looks like a genuine archaeological site, complete with a notice in three languages stating that the stretch of broken paving dates from about 39 BC. Not true. It was in fact placed here by Bijl in 1994.

369 **SURROUNDINGS**
Middelheim Park
Suburbs (Middelheim) ⑫

Located on the edge of the park close to the Braem Pavilion, Alik Cavaliere's *Omgeving* looks like a street of typical Belgian town houses. But these buildings are simply façades.

370 **ORBINO**
Middelheim Park
Suburbs (Middelheim) ⑫

Luc Deleu has transformed a stack of five shipping containers into a large installation. You can climb the steps to enter the top two containers, where art is exhibited.

MIDDELHEIM STATUES

The 5 most
UNUSUAL STATUES

371 PEPTO BISMO
Sint Jansplein
Antwerpen-Noord ⑨

It's worth making a detour to Sint Jansplein to look at the curious sculpture of a flying man titled *Pepto Bismo*. This bronze Icarus – with propellers instead of wings – was donated in 2003 by the Antwerp artist Panamarenko. A second version stands on top of a new office building in the old town, at the corner of Tabakvest and Baeckelmansstraat (best seen from outside Langegang 27).

372 FREE SCHELDT
Marnixplaats
Het Zuid ②

The enormous statue in the middle of Marnixplein was built in 1883 to celebrate the 20th anniversary of the treaty that opened the Scheldt to shipping. It is designed in a truly epic style, with sea gods, snapping chains and ship's prows.

373 BLANCHE DE FRANCE

Lange Gasthuisstraat 19
Central Antwerp ①
+32 (0)3 338 81 88
www.mayervandenbergh.be

The Museum Mayer van den Bergh owns a tiny sculptured head of Blanche de France, daughter of the King of France, who died before her third birthday, just 17 days after her sister's death. The King was devastated and commissioned a marble tomb with the figures of his two daughters. It was destroyed in the French Revolution, leaving just one sad head of a girl in a deserted Antwerp museum.

374 THE MAN WHO MEASURES THE CLOUDS

Desguinlei 25
Southern Antwerp ⑦

Jan Fabre's bronze statue *The Man Who Measures the Clouds* was placed on the roof of De Singel art centre in 1999. The sculpture shows a man standing on a library ladder while he reaches up with a school ruler to calculate the size of the clouds. "The figure symbolises my trade," Fabre once explained.

375 DAVID

Den Brandt Park
Beukenlaan
Suburbs (Middelheim) ⑬

A lifesize statue of Michelangelo's David stands in a corner of Den Brandt Park surrounded by an iron fence. There is nothing to explain how it arrived here. The story is that it originally stood outside the Italian pavilion at the 1910 Brussels World Fair and was later moved to this park.

SWEETIE DARLING

15 THINGS TO DO WITH CHILDREN

The 5 most fun activities for
SMALL CHILDREN

376 **NACHTEGALEN PARK**
Floraliënlaan 115
Suburbs (Middelheim) ⑫

The romantic-sounding *Nachtegalen Park*, or Nightingale Park, has a large adventure playground where kids can climb and dig while their parents sit on the terrace of De Melkerij. When the kids get hungry they can pick up a hot dog at a little wooden cabin.

377 **HET PALEIS**
Theaterplein
Central Antwerp ①
+32 (0)3 202 83 60
www.hetpaleis.be

This is an imaginative city theatre where most productions are aimed at children. The programme includes plays, readings and concerts. Children who share the same name as the director of the performance get admitted free.

378 **MUZZZE**
Middelheim Park
Suburbs (Middelheim) ⑫
+32 (0)3 288 33 60
www.middelheimmuseum.be

Look out for the rows of colourful suitcases hanging from racks at the entrance to Middelheim sculpture park. You pick up a suitcase in the colour corresponding to your child's age, ranging from five to 11 years. It will contain puzzles, games and information on five sculptures in the park.

379 HET STEEN DER WIJZEN

Steenplein 1
Central Antwerp ①
+32 (0)3 202 83 80
www.hetpaleis.be

The old castle Het Steen on the Scheldt waterfront has been reinvented as a children's activity centre. Designed by Het Paleis theatre company, it aims to entertain and inspire young children with games, exhibitions, workshops and a rooftop observatory.

380 DE STUDIO

Maarschalk
Gérardstraat 4
Central Antwerp ①
+32 (0)3 260 96 10
www.destudio.com

This theatre has a programme of activities for children, neatly classified by age. The productions for the youngest kids, aged 0-3, are often without words. Shows for older kids will usually be in Dutch.

The 5 best
SHOPS FOR KIDS

---

381 IN DEN OLIFANT
Leopoldstraat 23
Central Antwerp ①
+32 (0)3 231 61 14
www.indenolifant.be

Nelly and Hilde run a delightful toy shop in a former notary's office opposite the botanical gardens. The little rooms have been transformed into enchanting spaces, filled with story books or containing a miniature circus.

382 SJOKKEL
Wijngaardstraat 4
Central Antwerp ①
+32 (0)3 234 28 27

Everyone falls in love with Jetty De Laet's cluttered toy shop. Located on a narrow cobbled lane, the shop is crammed with music boxes, wooden tractors, porcelain tea sets and tin trains.

383 SWEETIE DARLING
Vleminckveld 8
Central Antwerp ①
+32 (0)485 06 90 13
www.sweetiedarling.be

Eef Rombaut has created an inspiring kids' concept store where she stocks stunning clothes and shoes. She also hunts out curious toys, furniture and storybooks. The perfect place to pick up a present if your best friend has just become a parent.

384 DE GROENE WOLK

Korte Gasthuisstraat 22
Central Antwerp ①
+32 (0)3 234 18 47
www.degroenewolk.com

A friendly shop filled with colourful and original clothes for fashionable kids. You find amazing apparel by Belgian designers like Max & Lola, Atelier Assemblé and even Dries van Noten.

385 DE PRINSES OP DE ERWT

Graaf van Egmontstraat 1
Het Zuid ②
+32 (0)3 216 41 18
www.prinsesopdeerwt.be

Decorated with floral wallpaper like a little girl's bedroom, this is a fun place to shop for chic but practical kids' clothes. The name means 'The Princess on the Pea'. Should you come with a princess in tow, the shop has a small play area.

384 DE GROENE WOLK

383 SWEETIE DARLING

The 5 best places for
EATING WITH KIDS

386 **SENSUNIK**
Molenstraat 69
Southern Antwerp ⑦
+32 (0)3 216 00 66
www.sensunik.be

This is a place for parents to relax while their kids run around in an attic filled with wooden toys and games. The adult menu offers simple Belgian dishes such as mussels or steak and frites, while the little ones upstairs are fed roast chicken with apple sauce or spaghetti bolognaise.

387 **HET GELUK**
Het Paleis
Theaterplein
Central Antwerp ①

This busy, bright café located inside Het Paleis theatre is popular with actors and writers, but also parents with small children. It has vintage wooden chairs and red formica tables, while the terrace looks across the vast concrete expanse of Theaterplein.

388 **HET MISSVERSTAND**
Sint-Andriesplaats 17
Central Antwerp ①
+32 (0)3 234 05 36
www.hetmissverstand.be

Here is a friendly place to eat with kids. Located on a quiet city square, the atmosphere is informal while the menu offers simple food like tapas, pasta and salads. In the summer, you can sit outside at one of the long tables while your kids burn off energy in the playground just a few metres away.

389 **LUNCHBOX**
Nieuwstad 8
Central Antwerp ①
+32 (0)3 231 04 79
www.lunchbox.be

This bright green health food café is one of the friendliest places in town to eat with kids. The children's menu includes Belgian favourites like chicken with frites and apple sauce as well as Ben & Jerry's ice cream. But it can get terribly crowded when school is out.

390 **22B**
Sint-Vincentiusstraat 22B
Southern Antwerp ⑦
+32 (0)475 67 49 30
www.22b.be

This bright modern self-service café is located in a brick building that was once a diamond cutting factory. Friendly and busy, it attracts customers of all ages, from wifi surfing students to nurses from the local hospital. The menu includes salads, quiche and various sandwiches.

386 SENSUNIK

DE WITTE LELIE

25 PLACES
TO SLEEP

The 5 most
HIP HOTELS

---

391 DE WITTE LELIE
Keizerstraat 16
University Quarter ③
+32 (0)3 226 19 66
www.dewittelelie.be

Steven Spielberg, Madonna and Naomi Campbell have all slept in this beautiful 11-room hotel, located in three white 17th-century gable houses. Fashion buyers and design journalists immediately fall in love with the stone fireplaces, pale wood floors and plump white bedspreads.

392 JULIEN
Korte Nieuwstraat 24
Central Antwerp ①
+32 (0)3 229 06 00
www.hotel-julien.com

As discreet as a Dries van Noten shopping bag, this boutique hotel is located in two restored 18th century houses close to the Carolus Borromeuskerk. Its 21 rooms are furnished in a cool minimalist style that perfectly fits this city of fashion. There is also a little cobbled courtyard for sunny days, a large rooftop terrace and a spa.

393 PRINSE
Keizerstraat 63
University Quarter ③
+32 (0)3 226 40 50
www.hotelprinse.be

An elegant hotel located in a historic 16th century town house in the Keizerstraat. The 35 rooms are decorated in a cool contemporary style, some overlooking a secluded renaissance garden. Its room rates are often quite low.

394 MATELOTE

Haarstraat 11A
Central Antwerp ①
+32 (0)3 201 88 00
www.hotel-matelote.be

Located on a cobbled lane near the town hall, the Matelote provides just the right level of cool chic to keep the fashion crowd amused. The converted 17th century brick townhouse has a minimalist lobby, a relaxed bar with a blazing fire and 12 bedrooms designed in different styles by Peter Deelen.

395 LINDNER

Lange Kievitstraat 125
Station Quarter ④
+32 (0)3 227 77 00
www.lindner.de

Located in the redeveloped Kievitplein quarter next to Centraal Station, this hotel stands out for its contemporary design and friendly staff. The rooms are spacious and comfortable, with touches of contemporary design. Worth asking for a room on an upper floor for a good view of the city.

391 DE WITTE LELIE

The 5 most
STYLISH B&B'S

396 ROSIER 10

Rosier 10
Central Antwerp ①
+32 (0)489 27 99 99
www.rosier10.be

Rosanne Stevens has created a sublime B&B in a 19th century house in the heart of the old town. The four rooms are named Matin, Midi, Soir and Minuit, each with a style to fit the name. So Morning is white and clean, while Midnight is dark and sexy.

397 ROOM NATIONAL

Nationalestraat 24
Central Antwerp ①
+32 (0)473 73 56 50
www.roomnational.be

The fashion sisters Violetta and Vera Pepa have created a cool B&B above a shop near the fashion museum. Room 01 has a minimalist look, with bare wooden floors and a separate little bedroom, while room 69 is decorated in the style of the 1960s. No breakfast here, but there are good cafés all around.

398 LINNEN

Lijnwaadmarkt 9
Central Antwerp ①
+32 (0)475 76 30 74
www.cocktailsatnine.be

Located under the Cathedral spire, this urban hideaway occupies an 18th century town house with a cocktail bar on the ground floor. The three guest rooms are decorated in a warm contemporary style that blends well with the historic architecture.

399 YELLOW SUBMARINE

Falconplein 51
University Quarter ③
+32 (0)475 59 59 83
www.yellowsubmarine.be

The Falconplein used to be a dodgy neighbourhood, but it has lately become quite fashionable. You can see this for yourself if you stay at this stylish B&B. It has three rooms furnished in a cool minimalist style. Elke Urbain ensures her guests have everything they need.

400 LUXE SUITES STUDIO 1-2-3

Lange Lozanastraat 16
Southern Antwerp ⑦
+32 (0)3 226 35 52
www.studios123.be

Davy Brocatus and Anatoly Nefedov have created a stylish B&B above their dance studio in southern Antwerp. The two suites are spacious and stylish, with separate kitchens and a terrace. The rooms are equipped with everything you might need, including fresh flowers, bath robes and toothbrushes.

399 YELLOW SUBMARINE

The 5 best
SMALL HOTELS

401 'T SANDT
Zand 13-19
Central Antwerp ①
+ 32 (0)3 232 93 90
www.hotel-sandt.be

Here is the ideal small hotel, located in a former 19th century fruit warehouse. Bedrooms are spacious and stylish, each decorated in a different style (including some tucked under the eaves). Add an Italianate garden, rooftop terrace and a location close to the Scheldt, and you have one of the most appealing small hotels in the city.

402 LE TISSU
Brialmontlei 2
Jewish Quarter ⑤
+32 (0)3 281 67 70
www.le-tissu.be

A perfect small hotel – just five rooms – located in a former parsonage next to a church. The interiors were decorated by two Antwerp designers who have their office in the building. They have gone for a deeply romantic style using a rich variety of fabrics (giving the hotel its name, The Fabric).

403 HOTEL ELZENVELD
Lange Gasthuisstraat 45
Central Antwerp ①
+32 (0)3 202 77 71
www.elzenveld.be

Here is a secret hotel hidden within the walls of an ancient hospital dating back to the 15th century. The bedrooms are quite sober, but the enclosed garden is romantic and the location is perfect for wandering around the old town.

404 FIREAN

Karel Oomsstraat 6
Southern Antwerp ⑦
+32 (0)3 237 02 60
www.hotelfirean.com

A charming family-run hotel in an Art Deco mansion dating from 1929. The garden is spacious and breakfast is generous. Located in a residential neighbourhood, it is a 20-minute tram ride from the centre, but within walking distance of Middelheim sculpture park.

405 HOTEL O

Handschoenmarkt 3
Central Antwerp ①
+32 (0)3 500 89 50
www.hotelhotelo.com

This is a friendly designer hotel located on a small square opposite the Cathedral. The interiors were designed by the Antwerp architect Jo Peeters, who went for black walls. The location could hardly be better, although the square outside is inevitably noisy at night.

The 5 best lodgings for a
ROOM WITH A VIEW

406 AAN DE LEIEN
Britselei 49/6
Southern Antwerp ⑦
+32 (0)3 288 66 95

This B&B has three rooms available, two of them relatively small (and not too expensive), but the one everyone wants is the sublime penthouse apartment. This vast living space has stone floors and a rooftop decked terrace with views of the city skyline.

407 B&B ATELIER 20
Sint-Paulusstraat 20
Central Antwerp ①
+32 (0)479 74 14 55
www.atelier20.be

Nathalie's stylish B&B lies in the heart of the historic Sint Paulus quarter. The suites are large and light, with interesting views of the old city. Nathalie is exceptionally friendly and delivers a generous Continental breakfast to your room.

408 SCHELDEZICHT
Sint-Jansvliet 10-12
Central Antwerp ①
+32 (0)3 231 66 02
www.hotelscheldezicht.be

This family-run hotel is a great place to stay if you are travelling on a budget. But don't be deceived by the name Scheldezicht (Scheldt View). The view you get (if you pay for a room at the front) takes in a little square, but no river. It has the feel of a family hotel, with old photographs and books everywhere.

409 COCO-MAT RESIDENCE

De Keyserlei 11
Station Quarter ④
+32 (0)3 231 68 06
www.antwerp.coco-mat-
hotels.com

Several smart urban apartments have been created in a corner building on de Keyserlei. They are large, with oak floors and comfortable sofas. It's worth paying a little extra for the penthouse apartment on the 6th floor which has a terrace with a spectacular view of the city. Be sure to let them know if you are arriving after 6 pm.

410 KOOL KAAI

Kleine Kraaiwijk 1
Central Antwerp ①
+32 (0)473 91 64 83
www.kool-kaai.com

Sarah and Perry have created a stylish B&B in a modern corner house. We love the duplex room on the top two floors, with a long wooden deck looking out on the river and the Sint Pauluskerk. The owners pay attention to the little details, like leaving breakfast outside your door in a little basket.

The 5 most
UNUSUAL PLACES
to sleep

---

411 **BARKENTIJN MARJORIE**
Napoleon Kaai
Het Eilandje ⑧
+32 (0)475 24 54 28
www.marjorie2.com

Built in Germany in 1932, this three-masted ship was rebuilt as a hotel in 2001. The interior has been furnished in authentic style with wooden decks, shiny brass fittings and porthole windows. And the staff wear crisp white uniforms to complete the picture. Bedrooms are small but comfortable.

412 **DE WITTE NIJL**
Tolstraat 35
Het Zuid ②
+32 (0)3 336 26 85
www.dewittenijl.be

This beautiful 19th century town house has been decorated in a romantic Belgian colonial style to evoke a journey up the Congo River. There are just two rooms, named after Livingstone and Stanley. Breakfast is served in a conservatory with potted palms and memorabilia while the walled garden could be somewhere in Africa.

413 **BOULEVARD LEOPOLD**
Belgiëlei 135
Jewish Quarter ⑤
+32 (0)3 225 52 18
www.boulevard-leopold.be

Here is a grand Belgian town house from the opulent 1890s with original moulded ceilings, parquet floors and tiled bathrooms. The apartments, which sleep three, are truly magnificent, and breakfast is a special experience.

414 THE GLORIOUS INN

De Burburestraat 4a
Het Zuid ②
+32 (0)3 237 06 13
www.theglorious.be

A romantic B&B in the Zuid district with three dark and mysterious rooms furnished with four-poster beds, antique vases and old paintings. Even the bathrooms are stylish and quirky. The rooms are located above an excellent bistro and wine bar. Booking is essential at the weekends.

415 SOUL SUITES

Marnixplaats 14
Het Zuid ②
+32 (0)471 285 716
www.soulsuites.com

This unusual residence on the hip Marnixplein offers eight stylish and spacious apartments. The rooms were designed by Jeanne van de Meulengraaf in a quirky vintage style that appeals to artists, writers and other bohemians.

415 SOUL SUITES

SWIMMING POOL IN BOEKENBERG PARK

40 ACTIVITIES
FOR WEEKENDS

———

The 5 best
WEEKEND WALKS

---

416 **ANTWERP HISTORY**
Grote Markt
Central Antwerp ①

For a walk in the historical town, begin on Grote Markt and follow Wissel- straat, then Oude Beurs, glancing into the courtyard at No. 16. At the end of the street, go left along Zirkstraat and then right to reach the Sint Pauluskerk. Take time to explore the church and its strange garden before crossing the Vee- markt and turning down Peterseliestraat. This leads to the Burchtgracht, which follows the line of the city moat passing below the Vleeshuis, where fragments of the city wall have survived.

417 **WATERFRONT**
Hanzestedenplaats 1
Het Eilandje ⑧
+32 (0)3 338 44 34
www.mas.be

For a perfect Sunday morning walk, begin with brunch at Storm, the MAS museum café, then follow the quays into town. At the Zuiderterras café, cross the road to the pedestrian tunnel and walk through to reach the Left Bank. Turn right and follow the waterfront until you come to the windmill on the bend in the river. Here you find several restaurants that make perfect lunch spots.

417 STORM

ANTWERPEN

417 ZUIDERTERRAS

418 CLIN IC

418 **FASHION**
Groenplaats
Central Antwerp ①

Begin the walk on Groenplaats and head down Nationalestraat to visit the fashion museum MoMu. Cross the road and head down Kammenstraat for a mix of edgy youth fashion and elegant accessories. Turn right down IJzerenwaag to visit the Scandinavian concept store Moose in the City. At the end of the street, go left down Nationalestraat and continue down Volkstraat where you can stop for coffee at Caffè Internazionale. Continue to Leopold de Waelstraat and turn down the third street on the right, De Burburestraat, to reach the concept stores Clinic and Hospital. Turn right on Vlaamse Kaai to end the walk at the concept store Your.

419 **ARCHITECTURE AND DESIGN**
Koningin Astridplein 27
Station Quarter ④

Begin in the main hall of Centraal Station to admire the magnificent architecture, then walk through the building to Kievitplein, a renovated square bordered by the 19th century railway viaduct and the back wall of the zoo. The British artist Richard Woods painted bright red and green bricks on several old buildings, transforming a dingy neighbourhood into a fun space. Walk around the zoo following Ploegstraat and Ommeganckstraat then cross Carnotstraat. Turn left and go up the second street on the right to reach the striking new design centre De Winkelhaak. End the walk in the Atelier Solarshop opposite.

420 COGELS OSYLEI

Tramplein 1
Zurenborg ⑥

This walk takes you through an area of stunning late 19th century architecture. Take tram 11 to the Tramplein stop to begin the walk, and go down Cogels Osylei. Among the remarkable buildings, notice the flamboyant group at No. 17 by Joseph Bascourt, a prolific architect who designed 25 houses in the quarter. At the end of the street, turn right along Guldenvliesstraat and then right again on Waterloostraat, where the houses at No. 11 and No. 30 celebrate the Battle of Waterloo. At the end of the street, turn right along Transvaalstraat to get back to Tramplein.

419 CENTRAL STATION

420 COGELS OSYLEI

The 5 best
CITY PARKS

---

421 **PARK SPOOR NOORD**
Viaduct-Dam 2
Antwerpen-Noord ⑨

This 1.6 km long park occupies an abandoned railway marshalling yard in the north of the city. The derelict train sheds have been restored and urban wasteland turned into green space. The park offers endless activities including a jogging trail and a children's playground. Come here on a summer evening and you will find pop up bars serving ice cold beer.

422 **STADSPARK**
Rubenslei
Jewish Quarter ⑤

A romantic 19th century park, the Stadspark was laid out on the site of a 16th century fortress. The winding paths lead to interesting statues and a romantic war memorial. Look out for the empty plinth where contemporary works are placed.

423 **BOEKENBERG**
Eksterlaan 3
Suburbs (Deurne) ⑫

This romantic park was once a country estate with a 19th century folly garden. The park also has a children's playground divided into four age categories, a café and an open air pool.

424 WOLVENBERG
Posthofbrug
Suburbs (Berchem) ⑫

Enclosed on all sides by busy roads, this wilderness near Berchem Station is not too easy to reach. Once you have crossed the busy road, you discover an untouched area of woodland, ponds and meandering trails. You might even forget that there is a roaring motorway just beyond the trees.

425 FORT 6
Universiteitsplein 1
Suburbs (Wilrijk) ⑫

The military engineer Henri Brialmont built a series of eight forts around Antwerp in the 19th century. It was a massive undertaking that took five years and 13,000 workers, but the forts failed to protect Antwerp when the German army invaded in 1914. Abandoned long ago, they have become unexpected nature reserves.

421 PARK SPOOR NOORD

The 5 strangest
WATERFRONT
LOCATIONS

---

426 SINT-ANNASTRAND
Wandeldijk
Left Bank ⑬

A stretch of beach lies just around the bend in the river on the left bank of the Scheldt. This became a fashionable resort in the 1930s. People still come here to eat in the restaurants behind the sea wall, swim in the open-air pool and cycle. But the casino has vanished, along with the beach huts and night clubs.

427 PIER
Steenplein
Central Antwerp ①

A new pier was built on the river in 2008 to replace an older structure that had decayed. This huge waterside deck has become a popular meeting place where students sit on summer afternoons and couples come to watch the sun set.

428 WELVAERT
Bonapartedok
Het Eilandje ⑧

A little floating urban garden has been created around an old crane standing on two pontoons next to the MAS. The artists' collective TimeCircus cultivates bamboo, grows vegetables and keeps a few chickens. It is all part of a temporary experiment in urban living that includes a café and performances. The project is due to run until 2014.

429 11 CRANES

Rijnkaai, near Hangar 27
Het Eilandje ⑧
www.havenkranen.be

It is a bit of a hike to reach the collection of 11 harbour cranes that stands on the Scheldt quayside. These giant machines were once used to unload ships in the Antwerp docks.

430 CRUISE TERMINAL

Ernest Van Dijckkaai
Central Antwerp ①

The new Cruise Terminal is hidden under the promenade that runs between Steenplein and Zuiderterras. Built in 2003, it allows giant cruise ships to moor close to the city centre.

The 5 best
SWIMMING POOLS

431 BADBOOT

Kaai 20
Kattendijkdok
Het Eilandje ⑧
www.badboot.be

A large open-air swimming pool floats in the Kattendijk dock near the MAS museum. Opened in 2012, the pool has some smart ecological innovations, including an area planted with reeds to purify the water, along with two sun decks and a brasserie. In winter, it is turned into a skating rink.

432 VELDSTRAAT

Veldstraat 83
Antwerpen-Noord ⑨
+32 (0)3 290 55 55

Here is a beautiful Art Deco swimming pool that is gleaming like new after an extensive renovation. It opened in 1933 to serve a poor working class district. The building is a masterpiece of modernism, with stained glass, neon lighting and energy-saving heating. It now also has a stylish hammam.

433 BOEKENBERG

Park Boekenberg
Van Baurscheitlaan
Suburbs (Deurne) ⑫
+32 (0)3 411 19 95

The open-air pool in the Boekenberg Park was converted in 2007 into the country's first eco swimming pool. German landscape architects Dongus lined the pool floor with more than 22,000 aquatic plants to maintain the water purity. It is now one of the most appealing pools but it can get crowded.

434 WEZENBERG

Desguinlei 17
Southern Antwerp ⑦
+32 (0)3 259 23 11

This modern indoor Olympic pool on the south side of town attracts serious lap swimmers. As well as the 50-metre pool (often used for competitions), it has a small pool where children can learn.

435 DE MOLEN

Wandeldijk 40
Left Bank ⑪
+32 (0)3 219 10 36

This is a huge open air pool on the Left Bank where you can swim next to the river. Opened in the 1930s near an old windmill, the Olympic-size pool is marked out for lane swimming. The cafés and restaurants on Sint-Anna beach are nearby.

433 BOEKENBERG

The 5 most inspiring ways to
PARTY AFTER DARK

—————

436 SCHELD'APEN

D'Herbouvillekaai 36
Southern Antwerp ⑦
+32 (0)3 238 23 32
www.scheldapen.be

It started in 1999 when a group of alternative artists and musicians took over an abandoned industrial site near the edge of the city. Now Scheld'Apen have moved into an abandoned villa and became a little more mainstream. But you still find wild parties, cheap vegetarian food, concerts by new bands and shows by emerging artists. They will have to move on again in a few years, so enjoy the anarchy while it lasts.

437 MAGIC CLUB

Desguinlei 94
Southern Antwerp ⑦
+32 479 910 800
www.wearemagic.be

A small 1980s disco in the lower basement of the Ramada Plaza Hotel has been brought back to life. So you can dance to old hits by Madonna and Queen while floor tiles flash and glitter balls spin overhead. The Saturday night parties attract a friendly crowd who know how to party. Reservation is required.

438 RED & BLUE

Lange Schippers-
kapelstraat 11
University Quarter ③
+32 (0)3 213 05 55
www.redandblue.be

Antwerp's coolest gay club is located in the heart of the red light district. This place is all about flamboyant fun. The famed Saturday night events are exclusively male, but women get to rule the place once a month during Café de Love evenings, while everyone can join the fun at the occasional Studio 54 themed parties.

439 CAFÉ D'ANVERS

Verversrui 15
University Quarter ③
+32 (0)3 226 38 70
www.café-d-anvers.com

Café d'Anvers organises wild underground dance parties in the heart of the red light district. Housed in a 16th century church, the club can hold up to 800 people. Students pack in here on Thursday nights to dance to electro, techno and house, while an older crowd fills the place on Saturdays.

440 FLYING SAUCERS ARE REAL

www.fsar.be

The people behind Flying Saucers are Real organise occasional pop-up dance parties in unexpected locations. Previous events have been staged in the MAS museum café and the old castle on the waterfront. As well as DJs playing rare vinyl, they occasionally present new bands and theatre performances.

The 5 best places to hear
GOOD MUSIC

---

441 TRIX
Noordersingel 28
Borgerhout ⑲
+32 (0)3 670 09 00
www.trixonline.be

This striking music venue is located on the edge of town between the ring motorway and the railway line to the Netherlands. But it is worth the journey to catch new bands performing in front of a friendly crowd. The venue also hosts music classes and invites musicians to talk about their playlists.

442 PEKFABRIEK
Kattenberg 93
Borgerhout ⑲

No website. No phone. No programme. So you have to rely on word of mouth to find out what's happening here. Hidden down a cobbled lane in Borgerhout, this converted factory recalls the anarchic energy of the 1970s. Emerging Antwerp bands and DJs perform in a raw industrial space lit by neon lights, while the Antwerp band dEUS rehearses in an upstairs studio. The Plaza Real bar next door is run by dEUS violinist Klaas Janzoons.

443 DE KLEINE HEDONIST

Sint-Jacobsmarkt 34
University Quarter ③
+32 (0)494 82 02 68
www.dekleinehedonist.be

You could easily walk past this café, but take a look inside (if it is open). You enter a large room on two levels with armchairs and tables scattered around. This is a good place to head if you are looking for a concert, or a TEDx debate, or a poetry reading, or just a place to think.

444 AMUZ

Kammenstraat 81
Central Antwerp ①
+32 (0)3 292 36 80
www.amuz.be

This beautiful old baroque chapel that once belonged to an Augustinian monastery has been carefully restored as a venue for classical concerts played on historic instruments. The entrance may look modern, but just wait until you see the dazzling neo-Byzantine frescos in the side chapel.

445 PIANO PAUL

Meir 52
Central Antwerp ①

A street musician called Piano Paul plays blues and rock 'n' roll on an old piano on wheels. He moves the piano across town by bicycle and performs on the main shopping street, Meir.

The 5 best
SUMMER FESTIVALS

---

446 LAUNDRY DAY
Ledeganckkaai
Southern Antwerp ⑦
www.laundryday.be

The secret is out now. When Laundry Day started in 1998, it was a modest street party in the Kammenstraat with lines of laundry hung from the buildings. Now it has grown into a cool techno festival that attracts more than 50,000 people to an abandoned industrial site. But it is still enormous fun.

447 JAZZ MIDDELHEIM
Beukenlaan 12
Suburbs (Middelheim) ⑫
www.jazzmiddelheim.be

A summer jazz festival is held in August among the trees in Den Brandt park, not far from Middelheim sculpture park. Founded back in 1969, Middelheim attracts serious jazz fans from all over Europe. The atmosphere is relaxed, with performers playing under a big tent while fans sit around on the grass drinking chilled white wine.

448 ZOMER VAN ANTWERPEN

+32 (0)3 224 85 20
www.zomervanantwerpen.be

An inspiring festival that fills the months of July and August, and reaches into the most remote corners of the city. Parties happen in a former gasworks in Zurenborg, now called Zomerfabriek, while Cinema Urbana screens open-air films in a disused hangar on the waterfront. But you can also have drinks with friends under the trees at the Zomerbar, or you can find circus acts, street theatre and pop up hotel rooms that cost next to nothing.

449 TOMORROWLAND

De Schorre
Boom
www.tomorrowland.be

Some 180,000 fans of electronic music arrive from all over the world for this festival, which happens in the quiet little town of Boom. Voted the world's best electronic festival in 2013, Tomorrowland occupies a huge site decorated like a Disney theme park.

450 SUMMERFESTIVAL

Ledeganckkaai
Southern Antwerp ⑦
www.summerfestival.be

Held at the start of the summer, this two-day music festival takes place on a big site in the south of the city. It features dozens of DJs pumping out sounds on eight different stages.

The 5 best
ANTWERP FILMS

---

451 LOFT
Cockerillkaai 16
Het Zuid ②

This stylish 2008 thriller directed by Erik Van Looy tells the story of five rich Antwerp businessmen who share a waterfront loft apartment for illicit affairs. But their successful lives fall apart when a woman is found murdered in the apartment. Van Looy set his thriller in the striking Hoopnatie building designed by Conix Architects on the Scheldt waterfront and recently filmed a US version in New Orleans.

452 LINKEROEVER
Left Bank ⑪

This dark psychological thriller filmed by Pieter van Hees in 2008 takes its name from the bleak Left Bank of the river Scheldt. The story involves a young woman suffering from a nervous breakdown who moves with her boyfriend into a sinister apartment in a crumbling tower block. The filming skilfully captures the desolation of the Linkeroever, which has been a place of exile and execution since the Middle Ages.

453 DE ZAAK ALZHEIMER

Kattendijkbrug
Het Eilandje ⑧

An elderly serial killer suffers from Alzheimer's Disease in this stylish 2005 crime thriller directed by Erik Van Looy (released in the US as *The Alzheimer Case*). The killer is pursued by two detectives from the Antwerp police department through some striking Antwerp locations, including the northern docklands.

454 ANY WAY THE WIND BLOWS

Sint Jansvliet
Central Antwerp ①

This atmospheric 2003 film shot in Antwerp tells the stories of various locals wandering the streets and quaysides of the city. It was written and directed by dEUS singer Tom Barman and features a stylish opening sequence shot in the Sint-Anna Tunnel.

455 ANTWERP-CENTRAL

Astridplein
Station Quarter ④

An intriguing 2011 film by Peter Krüger inspired by W.G. Sebald's novel *Austerlitz*. Filmed in Antwerp's Central Station in magical realist style, it explores the grandeur of the station architecture and the history of its construction.

MAS

45 RANDOM FACTS AND URBAN DETAILS

5 *famous people*
BORN IN ANTWERP

---

456 JAN FABRE

Born in Antwerp in 1958, Jan Fabre is one of Europe's most exciting contemporary artists. But he is also one of the most controversial. He shocked people in Ghent in 2000 when he covered the classical columns of a university building with raw ham, and became a hate figure in 2012 when he made a short film showing cats being thrown in the air on the steps of Antwerp town hall.

457 SIDI LARBI CHERKAOUI

His father is Moroccan, his mother is Belgian and he was born in Antwerp in 1976. After spending time in New York and London, he returned to Belgium to set up his own company called *Eastman*, and put on a production called *Babel* (you can watch it on YouTube) that involved 18 performers from 13 countries speaking 15 languages. The result, said *The Guardian*'s critic, was "the most fiercely resonant dance theatre of the decade"

458 ABRAHAM ORTELIUS

Born in Antwerp in 1527, Abraham Ortelius was geographer to King Philip II of Spain. He travelled widely in Europe and published several maps in Antwerp, as well as the world's first atlas. Ortelius was the first geographer to advance the theory that the continents of Africa and America were once joined together.

459 MATTHIAS SCHOENAERTS

Born in Antwerp in 1977, Matthias Schoenaerts is one of the hottest acting talents around. After studying at Antwerp drama academy, he played a cheating husband in *Loft* and a bouncer in the French film *Rust and Bone*. He continues to live in Antwerp's unglamorous Borgerhout district.

460 LUC TUYMANS

Godtsstraat 15
Borgerhout ⑩
+32 (0)3 216 38 88
www.zeno-x.com

Born in an Antwerp suburb in 1958, the artist Luc Tuymans has always drawn inspiration from the darker periods of European history. One of his earliest works, a watercolour titled *Gas Chamber*, was based on Dachau concentration camp. He has also confronted Belgium's colonial past in several works. His paintings now sell for huge sums, but Tuymans still paints in a studio in Antwerp and exhibits at Zeno X Gallery.

The 5 most promising
YOUNG DESIGNERS

---

461 LENNY LELEU
www.lennyleleu.com

Lenny Leleu has been gaining attention recently for her sexy swimwear collections inspired by environmental disasters. The German-born designer studied fashion at the Antwerp Academy and designs strange voluminous clothes with a futuristic edge.

462 ANNECHIEN SMOLDERS
www.sixhugsandrocknroll.be

Annechien Smolders is a young graphic designer who recently started creating cool clothes for little kids. Inspired by rock bands and street art, she designs fun clothes for messing around.

463 JAN-JAN VAN ESSCHE
www.janjanvanessche.com

Jan-Jan van Essche is a 2003 graduate of Antwerp Academy who designs clothes for men featuring beautiful fabrics and layered constructions. He encourages his customers to buy a single layered collection that can be adapted as the seasons change.

464 SOFIE CLAES

www.wolfbysofieclaes.com

The young designer Sofie Claes gained rave reviews in fashion magazines for her *Wolf* collection. Inspired by the minimalism of Ann Demeulemeester, she designs simple black dresses with just a touch of quirkiness. She explains that she chose the name wolf because she designs for women who are "mysterious and a little bit masculine".

465 KAROLIEN VERSTRAETEN

Kaasstraat 2
Central Antwerp ①
+32 (0)486 948 558
www.karolienverstraeten.com

Karolien Verstraeten studied architecture before enrolling at the Antwerp Academy. She recently opened her own shop in a cobbled lane behind the town hall where she sells classy clothes for city streets.

The 5 best places to understand
ANTWERP'S HISTORY

---

466 **MAS**
Hanzestedenplaats 1
Het Eilandje ⑧
+ 32 (0)3 338 44 34
www.mas.be

The 60-metre MAS museum tower rises above the northern docks like a badly-stacked pile of red shipping containers. The history of the city is imaginatively presented here through a spectacular collection of model ships, paintings, old photographs and historic films.

467 **CITY WALL**
Vleeshuisstraat 7
Central Antwerp ①

The oldest city wall, a rugged stone structure, was torn down in the 19th century, but three surviving fragments can be tracked down. The most visible section can be seen attached to the wall of the old castle, Het Steen. The other two sections are a little harder to find – a stretch of stone wall runs next to a modern apartment building in Vleeshuisstraat, while another section crops up on the other side of the street, forming the rear wall of an old house.

468 NUCLEAR SHELTERS

Napoleonkaai
Het Eilandje ⑧

The city is dotted with almost 100 secret atomic bunkers built in 1955 during the Cold War when Antwerp's port was a strategic target. The bunkers are hidden deep below the quays, but the abandoned concrete entrances can sometimes be spotted in the port area.

469 FELIX ARCHIVES

Oudeleeuwenrui 29
Het Eilandje ⑧
+32 (0)3 338 94 11
www.felixarchief.be

The city archives present exhibitions on urban history on the ground floor of the 1861 St Felix warehouse. These small but fascinating exhibitions draw on the archive's vast collection of photos, maps and relics. Entry is free.

470 RED STAR LINE MUSEUM

Montevideostraat 3
Het Eilandje ⑧
+32 (0)3 206 03 50
www.redstarline.be

Millions of European emigrants sailed from Antwerp on Red Star Line steamers to start a new life in America. The crumbling brick sheds owned by the Red Star Line have been restored to create a museum of emigration, which opens on 27 September 2013.

The 5 most
IMPORTANT DATES
in Antwerp's history

---

471 20 MAY 1570
Kloosterstraat 11
Central Antwerp ①

On this day, the cartographer Abraham Ortelius published the world's first atlas. Titled *Theatrum Orbis Terrarum* (Theatre of the World), it contained 53 maps bound in a single book. Ortelius lived in Kloosterstraat, but not in the house that bears his name at No. 11.

472 4 NOVEMBER 1576

In an event that became known as the Spanish Fury, Philip II's troops rampaged through the streets of Antwerp. Thousands of citizens were murdered and many Protestants fled north to the Netherlands.

473 20 APRIL 1920
Atletenstraat 80
Suburbs (Kiel) ⑫
www.beerschot.be

In recognition of Belgium's suffering during the First World War, Antwerp was chosen to host the 1920 Olympics. The Olympic flag was flown for the first time at the Antwerp Games and doves were released into the sky to symbolise peace. The Olympic oath also dates from the 1920 games, which included a tug-of-war competition and diving in the city moat. The former Olympic stadium is now home to the local football team Beerschot AC.

474 16 DECEMBER 1944
De Keyserlei 15
Station Quarter ④

More than 500 people were killed on this day when a German V2 rocket hit the Rex Cinema near Central Station. Some 1,200 people were packed into the cinema watching The Plainsman when the rocket hit the building at 3.20 pm. Many of the dead were soldiers from the United States, Britain and Canada.

475 24 MARCH 1986
Nationalestraat 28
Central Antwerp ①
+32 (0)3 470 27 70
www.momu.be

On this day, six Antwerp designers presented their collections at London Fashion Week. They were all recent graduates of the Antwerp fashion school and had pooled their money to rent a van and share showroom space. The Antwerp designers won praise for their radical styles, but international journalists could not deal with the difficult Flemish names. So Walter van Beirendonck, Dries Van Noten, Dirk Van Saene, Marina Yee, Ann Demeulemeester and Dirk Bikkembergs became collectively known as the Antwerp Six.

The 5 most strange and unusual
URBAN DETAILS

476 DAM STATION
Damplein
Antwerpen-Noord ⑨

Dam Station is not in itself remarkable. It is a typical Flemish Renaissance brick building next to a railway viaduct. But what is unusual is that it was moved 36 metres in 1907 using an ingenious system of mechanical jacks and rails. This exceptional engineering project is commemorated by a series of enlarged old postcards displayed under the viaduct.

477 V2 WEATHERVANE
Heilige Geeststraat 25
Central Antwerp ①

Not many people have ever noticed the weathervane on top of a brick house opposite the Plantin Moretus Museum. It represents the V2 rocket that landed in the Vrijdagmarkt in 1944, destroying the house on this spot and damaging the Plantin Moretus Museum.

478 THE MAN IN THE WHITE DINNER JACKET
BEST SEEN FROM:
Cogels-Osylei 45
Zurenborg ⑥

A man in a white dinner jacket stands on the roof terrace of a house in the Zurenborg district. The ghostly figure was placed there by an events agency based in the building.

479 **GIRAFFENPLEIN**
Ploegstraat
Station Quarter ④

This is an unremarkable square at the back of the zoo. Or so you might think. But then you notice a giraffe's head poking above the brick wall. Other animals can sometimes be spotted through the windows set into the high wall on Ommeganckstraat.

480 **CITY STAFF UNIFORMS**

One of the original Antwerp Six, the bearded Walter van Beirendonck looks fearsome. Yet this wild designer was commissioned in 2003 to design uniforms for Antwerp's 1,900 city employees. Van Beirendonck decided to colour code the uniforms, so park keepers have green uniforms, street sweepers wear fluorescent yellow and museum guards wear brown.

476 **DAM STATION**

The 5 best
ANTWERP BANDS

481 **DEUS**

Founded more than 20 years ago, Antwerp's most famous band gained international attention with their debut album *Worst Case Scenario*. Fronted by Tom Barman, dEUS covers different styles from noisy rock to sad folksy ballads. Listen to *The End of Romances*.

482 **SCHOOL IS COOL**
www.schooliscool.be

Founded in 2009, this new baroque pop band from Antwerp perform pulsating dance songs that tell of teenage agony. They film video clips in unusual Antwerp locations on tiny budgets. Listen to *In Want of Something*.

483 **WAHWAHSDA**
www.wahwahsda.be

Here is a reggae band that has been producing an original mix of Flemish dialect rap and English rock lyrics since 2008. Their album *Radio Rum* came out in 2012. Listen to *Dinner for Two*.

484 **TOURIST**

The Antwerp reggae singer Tourist grew up in Antwerp's poor Stuyvenberg district. He raps in Antwerp dialect accompanied by swooning instrumentals. The songs often deal with the social problems of a multicultural city. Listen to *Mijn Stad*.

485 **DEZ MONA**
www.dezmona.com

This Antwerp band has been creating rich and dark sounds since they formed in 2003. They use rare instruments, piano and accordion to create astonishing compositions, including the strange 2012 song cycle *Sága*. The singer Gregory Frateur has one of the most haunting voices around. Listen to *Blue Girl*.

The 5 best
ANTWERP BLOGS

---

486 ANTWERPEN STREET STYLE
www.antwerpenstreetstyle. com

Twin sisters Helen and Tine and their friend Lara have been blogging on Antwerp street style for several years. They take to the cobbled streets with their digital cameras to capture the latest urban trends and interview people they like.

487 DOGS AND DRESSES
www.dogsanddresses.com

Elien is a smart Antwerp graduate who lives in Kammenstraat and blogs about clothes, shops and little cafés she finds. She has eclectic tastes in clothes, ranging from girly to rock.

488 FLEMISH FASHION FREAKS
www.flemishfashionfreaks. com

Established Antwerp fashion editor Ninette Murt and her daughter Nona Bludts publish this blog on fashion trends. Ninette, who founded Designers Against Aids, has some serious points to make about the fashion industry, beauty, charity and recycling.

489 ANTWERP FASHION OBSERVER
www.antwerpfashion-observer.blogspot.be

Two young women both called Géraldine curate this cool fashion blog on street styles. They have a growing team of contributors who photograph striking styles seen on the streets of Antwerp, Brussels and Ghent. The blog also lists fashion events across Belgium.

490 MOMU BLOG
blog.monu.be

This eclectic fashion blog is compiled by the people who work at Antwerp's fashion museum. The writers go behind the scenes at the museum to mull over illustrations in old fashion magazines, fashion in the movies and their favourite fashion people.

The 5 best words in
ANTWERP DIALECT

---

491 SINJOOR

The people of Antwerp have been called *Sinjoren* since the Spanish ruled the city in the 16th century. Derived from the Spanish word *señor*, the name suggests a certain aloof attitude. But not everyone in Antwerp is a *sinjoor*. It only applies to someone born within the 16th century city limits whose parents and grandparents were *sinjoren*. So almost no one can claim the name.

492 PAGADDER

This word dates from the Spanish period when *pagadores*, or paymasters, were short men rejected by the army. The word gradually became an affectionate term for children, and also for the lookout towers attached to merchant's houses (where children would be sent to watch for arriving ships).

493 BOLLEKE

Antwerp's De Koninck beer is served in a distinctive round glass called a *bolleke*, or little ball. So locals who want the city beer simply ask for a *bolleke*.

494 **ROGGEVERDOMMEKE**

Not an easy word to pronounce, *roggeverdommeke* is a rough raisin bread sold in Antwerp bakers. The name, so they say, derives from the 15th century when local monks baked bread for the poor. They also baked a coarse rye bread (rogge) destined for prisoners in the Steen, who were known as *verdomden*, or God forsaken.

495 **CABARDOESKE**

The word *cabardoeske*, meaning a seedy bar or brothel, dates from the period when the Napoleonic army occupied Antwerp. The French classified the local bars on a scale of one to 12, with the final category reserved for brothels. So the term *cabaret douze* was corrupted by the locals into the word *cabardoeske*.

The 5 best
ANTWERP BOOKS

---

496 CHEESE
MURAL LOCATED AT:
Sint-Pieter en Paulus-
straat
Central Antwerp ⓘ

Willem Elsschot's 1933 comic novella *Kaas* (Cheese) tells the story of Frans Laarmans, a clerk in an Antwerp shipping company who takes sick leave to launch a cheese importing company. He has no business sense, fritters away time trying to come up with a name for his company and finally has no idea what to do when 10,000 Edam cheeses are delivered to his home.

497 A DOG OF FLANDERS
PLAQUE LOCATED AT:
Handschoenmarkt
Central Antwerp ⓘ

Almost everyone in Japan knows the little children's book called *A Dog of Flanders*. Set in a village near Antwerp, it was published in 1874 by the British writer Louise de la Ramée and tells the story of a boy named Nello who saves the life of a dog called Patrasche. The boy wants to be an artist and dreams of seeing Rubens' *Descent from the Cross* in Antwerp Cathedral, but cannot afford the entrance fee. After enduring many hardships, he finally dies of hunger in front of the altarpiece, along with his dog.

498 ON BLACK SISTERS' STREET

LOCATED AT:
Zwartzustersstraat
Central Antwerp ①

Chika Unigwe's 2007 novel *Fata Morgana* looks at the lives of Nigerian women lured to Antwerp to work in the sex trade. The book is based on extensive research and interviews with African sex workers in Antwerp's red light district. Published in English under the title *On Black Sisters' Street*, it won the 2012 Nigerian Prize for Literature, the most important African literary award.

499 AUSTERLITZ

LOCATED IN:
Koningin Astridplein 26
Station Quarter ④

W.G. Sebald begins his great novel *Austerlitz* in Antwerp Central Station where the narrator meets a man from his past called Austerlitz. Sebald writes beautifully about the architecture of the station and the nocturnal animals in the nearby zoo. He also refers to the circle of 19th century fortifications around the city and the Nazi camp for political prisoners at Breendonk.

500 UTOPIA

HOUSE LOCATED IN:
Spanjepandsteeg
Central Antwerp ①

Thomas More published his political novella *Utopia* in 1516 following a visit to Antwerp. It begins with an account of a meeting in an Antwerp street with his friend Pieter Gilles, a city councillor. They went together to More's inn and sat in the garden to hear about Utopia from a sailor who had just returned from the imaginary island.

INDEX

COLOPHON

EDITING *and* COMPOSING – Derek Blyth

GRAPHIC DESIGN – Joke Gossé

PHOTOGRAPHY – Joram Van Holen (www.joramvanholen.be)

D/2013/12.005/2
ISBN 978 94 6058 1106
NUR 506

© 2013, Luster, Antwerp
www.lusterweb.com
info@lusterweb.com
Printed in Spain by Indice S.L. Arts gràfiques